10.95

D0893303

The Fish Book

The Fish Book

Jeffrey A. Fisher

Illustrations by John Silverio

Emerson Books, Inc.
Buchanan, N.Y. 10511

CONTENTS

To Uri Joseph Fisher, the son who rekindled the old meanings in my life.

To Susan Jo, the woman whose love made both this book and Uri possible.

PREFACE

As a boy I watched the men at the fishdocks catch, clean, cut,cut, buy and sell fish. I watched charter boat captains, commercial captains, fish buyers, dockside winos and homemakers as they came to make the family seafood purchase.

My first fishing trip came at age three, and I still remember how thrilled I was then. My uncle Joe, a fish master, was my professor and fish mentor, and my father lent his wisdom through the years.

I began fishing on my own when I was seven years old. When I was nine I would catch fish and sell them to the "weekend men" on Sunday afternoon so they could go home and, I'm sure, claim to have caught them. I caught and sold fish for spending money at age eleven. I started reading books about fish and finally wrote one of my own.

I have never stopped listening to others and learning their skills and tips on fish. In fact, most of what I know is information on loan from others, although I also have graduate degrees in fishery science. My interest in fish continues—a six-year-old son keeps rekindling old and pleasant fish flames in me.

With more learning, I hope someday to be a fish master. For the time being, I'm satisfied to be a fisherman and hope that this modest book will introduce you to this fascinating journey.

It is meant for the beginning fish person, but even an expert will pick up some new information, or find a different technique to try.

Not everyone will find my methods of catching, cleaning, preserving and preparing fish to be the best. There are other ways to conduct your affairs of fish, but the methodology in this book has worked for many through the years. It will give you some basic knowledge and then feel free to adapt the ideas to suit your needs. I'm always learning and changing my own methods; no reason you shouldn't do the same.

The reference lists included should pique your curiosity, if you want to do more research. And your local library will undoubtedly have even more information. Also note the Appendix at the back of the book for common sources of fish information.

Special thanks to a terrible fish person but excellent typist, niece Sherri Kurras.

From G.A. Bollore's "Guide de Pecheur a Pied": "Fishing is the oldest and most important human activity to which we owe our present existence." Twenty-five years from now, this may be the basis of your personal survival.

Author unknown: "Give a man a fish and he'll eat for a day. Teach a man to fish and he'll eat for a lifetime."

Fish people tell each other this one: "Be a fish person, and you'll be self-sufficient."

CHAPTER ONE
Be a Sport

Catching Fish for Recreation

These first two chapters introduce the beginner to the basics of sport and survival fishing. If you are an accomplished recreational or commercial fishing buff, feel free to skip on to the next chapters. Chances are you won't listen to advice anyway.

Sports fishing is a recreational activity motivated by pleasure. Generally the recreational angler uses basic rod, reel and hook tackle.

Commercial fishing is survival fishing, done for money or food, usually with mass-catching gear.

Sharp distinctions quickly break down. Many people who are fishing primarily for recreation, sell a portion of their catch to help offset trip expenses. And while they are ensuring themselves a livelihood, commercial people also enjoy fishing.

Fish people seek fish! And when the hunt is on, a bond exists between them that transcends religion, love, career, and politics.

The first rule for either recreational or commercial fishing is to dress properly. You're in, near or on the water when you're fishing, and it's always a little colder there in winter and a little hotter in summer. The wind moves more quickly across water and rain adds to the discomfort. A tolerable day at home can be a miserable one at sea. Dress warmly and wear layers, stay dry and be prepared to change clothing to suit Mother Nature. Nothing is more certain to take away all the pleasures of fishing than being wet or cold. Boots, rubberized rain gear and a wind breaker will prevent most of these problems. Loose clothing that won't restrict your movements—rowing, wading, boat handling and casting—is best.

Where to Fish—Broadly Speaking

Even the pros are always looking for fishing hot spots, which change as they are affected by fishing pressure and other environmental events.

A one acre trout lake that a million anglers visit every summer is under heavy fishing pressures. A lagoon visited only by a few gill net is under light pressure. More people, using more gear and making more trips may mean fewer fish for everyone.

Manmade or natural environmental events change the basic nature of the fishing spot. A new sewage outflow into a bay is a serious, negative event. A new sewage treatment plant is a very positive change. A new lakeshore housing development will probably change the character and productivity of that fishing area.

But every state in the union has areas that have always produced fish.

Here are a few hints to help you learn your area's fishing potential:

- Write to your state department of natural resources or conservation or to the fish and game service.
- Write to your state marine resources agency.
- Consult handbooks on fishing.
- Read books written by professionals in the fishing field.
- Consult outdoor magazines for special articles on where to go.
- Watch the pros in action.
- Ask to go along on commercial fishing ventures (offer to work for the privilege of watching pros fish).
- Talk with old-timers and other local people experienced in fishing.
- Talk with representatives from local offices of fish and game

agencies.
- Join a local fishing club.
- Read outdoor columns in local newspapers.
- Stay aware of special community projects, such as the construction of artificial reefs or a fishing pier.

Your best source of information is sure to be the locals, so don't be afraid to ask them for advice. Even the old pros were once beginners, and most people committed to the craft of fishing are happy to share their knowledge.

Where to Fish—Specifically

Most fish have favorite spots and repeatable habits that shift with the seasons. They prefer certain foods. They favor specific combinations of terrain, light, temperature, vegetation, etc. The moral: Know the preferences of the fish you are after, and vary your schedule, bait and locale to accommodate them.

Most fish that live on or very near the bottom of a river, lake, bay or ocean prefer obstructions in the form of rocks, wrecks, etc. Reefs and shellfish beds also attract large numbers of fish. Some fish, such as flounders, prefer either a clear sandy or a muddy bottom. Piers, docks, pilings, jetties, etc. also attract certain fish.

Bays and sounds—large bodies of water enclosed or semi-protected by land masses—often harbor large numbers of fish around grass flats, which are shallow areas with thick strands of marine grasses.

Try the mouth of a river, canal or creek.

At low tides or during temperature extremes try the deeper water such as inlets, channels or deep holes. Inlets are connections between large water bodies, such as the ocean, and small ones, such as the bay. Channels are natural or manmade deep pathways usually serving boat navigation. All of these spots are perfect for light spinning or bay fishing rods.

Offshore fishing is done in the deeper waters of large lakes, oceans, gulfs, etc., some distance from land. Great Lakes trout and Gulf of Mexico billfish are caught offshore.

In fishing offshore, constantly scan the surrounding waters. Look for dark patches, swirls, ripples, floating debris which attract fish.

Circling and diving sea birds are probably feeding on bait fish, so "go to the birds" when you can. On rough days you will have difficulty seeing fish, but when the water is calm, look for schools of bait fish.

In fishing fresh water, look for holes, stumps, floating vegetation, slight current, grass bottoms, marsh edges, etc. Knowing the behavior and habits of freshwater fish is probably more critical than knowing the habits of saltwater fish, since freshwater fish have more limited ranges, more demanding habits and fewer choices in meeting life needs. Think of saltwater fish as aggressive generalists and their freshwater relatives as specialists. Thus, if a brook trout feeds only on a particular May fly, you must fish with bait very similar to a May fly if you want to snag that trout. On the other hand, a feeding sea trout may be attracted to all sorts of baits: dead or live shrimp, cut strip bait, small crabs, worms, minnows and shiners, artificial lures, jigs, plugs, spoons and plastic baits.

Surf fishing is done standing on the shore of a large water body, such as an ocean beach and casting into the breaker waves, and it requires a special surf casting rod. To surf fish, look for dark water, which indicates depth. Fish near or between rocks. Fishing just *off* a sandbar is generally productive. Fish in early morning and evenings. Extremes in surf condition—flat calm or stormy rough—are not good fishing conditions. Fish areas with currents, holes, coves, cuts, sloughs, etc.

A clarifying note: Inshore fishing is done in bays, sounds, beaches, etc. closer to land than offshore fishing, but there is no precise definition of either term.

Bottom fishing is more specific. No matter where you are—lake, bay, gulf, sound, ocean—your bait is delivered to the bottom in search of those fish that live there.

Surf, bay, river, or open ocean fishing are more precise terms. You must be in those environments in order to fish in the style appropriate to them.

Among the common species of ocean, bay and fresh water fish:

Pacific Coast

Offshore fish include: lingcods, albacore and bluefish tuna, dolphin, swordfish, marlin, ocean perch and Pacific cod.

Inshore fish include: corbina, halibut, salmon, rockfish, mullet, mackerel, sheepshead, croaker and striped bass.

Some fish inhabit both offshore and inshore waters or move from one to the other seasonally, including flounders and soles, yellowtail, white sea bass, whitefish, shark, skate, and black cod.

Given the reputation for the unusual lifestyles of people on the West Coast, U.S.A. it is no surprise that there are aberrant fish as well. There is one fish on the West Coast that can be caught on land—the grunion. All that's required is a quick hand and a bucket.

Atlantic Coast

Inshore game fish include: pollock, black drum, shad, bluefish, channel bass, croaker, whiting, pompano, sea bass, sheepshead, snook, spotted sea trout, striped bass, flounder, fluke, weakfish, tautog, and scup.

Offshore varieties include: albacore, amberjack, ocean perch, sailfish, groupers, jewfish, marlin, tuna, mackerels, dolphin, snapper and swordfish.

Cobia, permit, sheepshead and groupers prefer reefs and underwater obstructions (rocks, wrecks, etc.).

Gulf Coast

Inshore fish that live in protected bays, harbors, bayous, and sounds, and are often found on grass flats, include: spotted sea trout, croaker, snook, bluefish and mullet.

Inshore fish that live directly in the Gulf of Mexico include: Spanish and king mackerel, cobia, pompano, white trout and jacks.

Offshore fish include: dolphin, sailfish and marlin on the surface, with triggerfish, snappers and groupers the dominant bottom fish. Redfish, croaker and tarpon are found in a variety of habitats.

Inland

Lake and river fishing in different parts of the United States yield different types of fish. Some popular freshwater fish are trout, bass, pike, pickerel and numerous smaller "panfish."

Rod and Reel Fishing

Most offshore fish are best caught by trolling, either with artificial lures or natural baits. Trolling takes place in a boat. The bait is pulled through the water while the boat moves. Your speed and the bait you use are the critical factors in trolling. When you are trolling for mackerel or bluefish, the boat moves only one to three miles per hour, but boat speed must be increased three times that to catch a tuna offshore.

Of the offshore varieties, flatfish—flukes, flounders, turbot, sole and halibut—are caught on the bottom with natural baits. "Flatfish" are just that: flattened bodies usually white on the underside and darker on top. Their shape and coloring makes them ideally suited for a bottom living existence. Other inshore fish can be caught with various artificial and natural baits, anywhere in the water column, from surface to bottom. Each species differs, so you've got to learn each of their idiosyncracies.

To go rod and reel fishing, you'll need a rod and reel, logically enough, in some sort of matched combination. You'll also need line and terminal tackle (hooks, swivels, sinkers, floats. etc.) and then you're all set. Go to the fishing equipment section of a sporting goods store or to a tackle shop and talk to the salesperson about the many combinations and possibilities. Most of them love fishing and relish the opportunity to make suggestions and advise you.

Your rod and reel combination will significantly determine the kind of fishing you can do. For example, a bait casting rod and reel is the best combination for bass fishing. Fly rods and reels are ideal for freshwater trout fishing. A matched rod, reel, line and rig combine to make the best way to catch a particular fish or group of similar kinds of fish. The following pages will get you started in the right direction.

A good, general classification of rod and reel combinations can be made on the basis of the type of casting they lend themselves to, and there are five types: spin, bait, surf, fly and bay (or boat).

Reels

The first saltwater reel had no drag and was aptly called a *knuckle buster*. C. F. Holder caught the first big game fish with the knuckle buster in 1898: a tuna that weighed 183 pounds. William Boscher developed the internal drag idea so the reel could take some of the pain out of fishing. J. Von Hofe and Joe Coxe manufactured the first saltwater reels with this drag mechanism in 1913.

The internal drag was an ingenious but necessary development. It can be likened to a brake on a car. Without a brake, a car races unimpeded down a hill, fast, erratic, and out of control, straining both driver and equipment. A hooked fish would wildly race off without internal drag, permitting the line to unwind from the reel spool in a swift, out-of-control, and taxing manner. By gently and carefully applying brake pressure to the careening car, the trip downhill becomes slower and more controlled. An internal drag on a fishing reel is a simple gearing mechanism that impedes the free unraveling of the line from the spool, giving the person fishing more control and making the fish work harder during the "run." The drag provides resistance and permits the reel to share the work of fighting the fish. Like a brake it can be tightened to impede spool movement entirely. The drag gives the angler more control over the strike and run of the fish.

Prior to this time, most saltwater sport fishing was done by dragline. The early reels were expensive so rod and reel fishing was for the rich. After World War I, better economic times put rod and reel fishing into the life of many more people.

Today, there are even electric reels, but these are not fitting for outdoors people. The modern reels are made of the highest quality plastics, rust-resistant metals and some of the newer lightweight materials.

Most modern reels need a minimum of care. Two things are usually sufficient: Wash the reel in fresh water after use and occasionally lubricate it. Fly reels require the least amount of care: Just give it an occasional drop of oil on the spindle. Bait casting, spinning and other saltwater reels need a little more attention. Lubrication points on these reels include spool spindles, gears, level wind mechanisms, metal bars that touch the line, pins and screws. Gears should be lightly greased; oil will suffice for all other parts. Special lubricants are available in fishing tackle stores.

Spinning Reels

The most distinctive feature about the spinning reel is that its spool is stationary. Thus, when casting, the line peels off the end freely. Other reels have a revolving spool that offers frictional resistance to the cast. The only force that pulls the line off a spinning reel spool is the weight of the tackle (sinker, lure, hook, etc.). When you're reeling in the line, the spool moves in and out, rather than revolving. The spool casing or cup revolves around the spool and guides the line back on to the spool. This ingenious idea was first put into practice in England by Holden Illingsworth, but was not brought to America until after World War II.

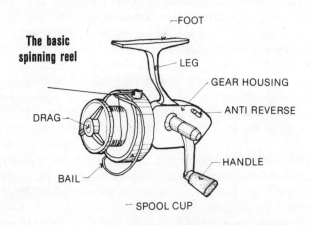

The basic spinning reel

—FOOT
LEG
GEAR HOUSING
ANTI REVERSE
DRAG
HANDLE
BAIL
— SPOOL CUP

The spool of the spinning reel will revolve only under one exceptional condition—if the pulling force of a fish exceeds the drag's brake setting. The tighter the drag, the larger the fish it will take to turn the spool. Spin reels now come in a variety of sizes and can be used for the lightest to the heaviest kind of fishing. Given their versatility for many kinds of fishing, strong construction, easy repair, interchangeable spools, compactness, reasonable price, and easy learning, I recommend this reel as your first buy. It serves equally well for fresh and saltwater fishing.

Spinning reels come with manual, automatic or bail line pick-up mechanisms. The bail model is recommended. A trip to a tackle shop will show you the differences clearly. The bail combines a metal ring and a small roller. Turning the reel's handle turns the bail, which retrieves and winds line on to the spool. To cast, an angler must "open" the bail to permit line to unravel from the spool freely.

Manual pick-ups have no bail but instead incorporate a simple roller mounted on the spool housing. The angler uses a fingertip to put the line on the spool (to retrieve the line) and off the roller (to cast).

Thus, the manual system requires more use of your hands.

Automatic pick-ups are curved arms (about half the length of the bail) which catch the line as you begin to retrieve it. It is a variation of the bail model.

Spinning reels are mounted under the rod, with the cranking handle usually on the left side, which is inconvenient for the left-handed caster. The reels do come in models with interchangeable or right-sided handles. Check these out if you cast with your left arm—it gets *very* tiring switching back and forth with every cast!

A major advantage of the spinning reel is interchangeable spools, which make it possible to change line in a few minutes to match the kind or size of fish you are catching. No other reel permits this. Like most reels, a drag (brake) is included, usually located on the face or front of the spool. Be sure the drag works smoothly, with no hesitation.

An offshoot of the spinning reel is the spin-casting reel. This reel has a push-button release (free spool) and the line is stored in a *housing* and is retrieved through the *nose cone,* which is a hole in the front of the housing. Buy the most expensive model you can find because many low cost but poorly built and unreliable spin cast reels are available. Also, before buying, be sure it matches your rod, because these reels don't fit all fishing rods.

Saltwater reels

The basic saltwater reel is best used for bottom fishing. Some call it a *boat reel* but it is as easily used from bridges, piers, shore, etc.

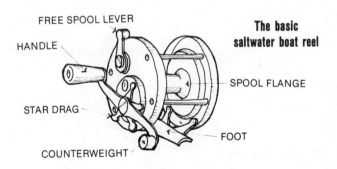

FREE SPOOL LEVER

HANDLE

STAR DRAG

COUNTERWEIGHT

The basic saltwater boat reel

SPOOL FLANGE

FOOT

Saltwater reels come in a wide range of sizes, which must be matched to your rod and the type of fish you are after. Good quality in a saltwater reel is essential: Sturdy construction, powerful drag and corrosion-resistant materials are musts. There are many models and makes. In similar price ranges, quality is about equal. Take your time choosing.

The surf-casting reel is quite similar to other saltwater reels, but has wider spool and specialized gears to permit distance casting from shore.

Modern trolling reels are nothing more than modified saltwater reels. They are bulkier and have very powerful drag mechanisms.

Bait-casting reels

The bait-casting reel is traditionally a freshwater reel but first-class saltwater anglers are using them increasingly more for big game fish. The bait-casting reel is a tribute to American ingenuity, with special thanks to a generation of Kentucky bass fishermen. George Snyder, a Paris, Kentucky bass fisherman, made the first working model shortly after 1800. J. Meek duplicated the Snyder reel and was manufacturing them by 1840. Other Kentucky bass fishermen improved the Meek product: J. W. Hardman and B. C. Milam replaced the rivets with high quality screws, and later the Shakespeare Company introduced their revolutionary "Marhoff" model incorporating a level-wind device. Meek bait-casting reels are now valuable antiques. James Heddon invented and produced an artificial bass plug that matched the performance of the reels. Freshwater fishing—especially bass fishing—hasn't slowed down since!

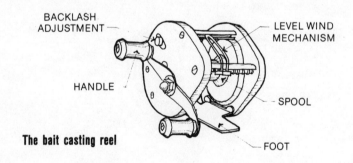

The bait casting reel

18

Today's bait-casting reels are precision-made from the highest quality materials and are relatively small. They perform flawlessly and make fishing a joy and a pleasure. They can even be used by non-Kentuckians—with extra practice of course!

Unlike the spinning reel, the bait-casting reels have a freely rotating spool. Release your thumb from the spool to complete a cast. Turn the handle to retrieve the line on the rotating spool again. Two things are required to cast well: a good machine and a good operator. The good machines are the expensive ones and the good operators are the practiced ones.

Fly-casting reels

While bait-casting reels were made for bass, fly-casting reels were made for trout. Saltwater anglers are also beginning to use the fly reel, which is relatively simple to operate and is available in a number of different models.

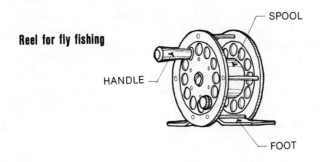

Reel for fly fishing

SPOOL

HANDLE

FOOT

Unlike other reels, most of the work in fighting a fish is left to your hands, the line and, most important, the fly rod. The fly reel is really just a place to keep your line so you don't trip. It taxes your fishing skill to the maximum.

A modern innovation is the automatic fly reel. Rather than trip on the line stored at your feet upon retrieval (if you can't manage to keep it all coiled in one hand), a triggering spring-operated device permits you to wind the line on the spool while you cast, fight a fish or eat a 10" pizza.

19

Rods

Fishing rods come in all shapes, sizes, weights and materials. Light spinning rods are 6′ to 7½′ long. Surf rods, from 7′ to 14′ long. Saltwater (boat) rods are generally 5′ to 7′ and bait casting rods are 5′ to 7′ long. The long, limber bait casting rods with a slightly extended butt or handle are now becoming popular in Florida saltwater fishing. Fly rods are long, narrow and extremely limber.

Rods are now made primarily of fiberglass and metal rods are also available. In years past, the material of choice was wood.

A rod is said to possess "action," in its whip, feel, balance, weight, stiffness and appearance. Anyone who fishes often enough learns how to use that action. Be patient, you too will learn!

A fishing rod must be matched with the reel, as already explained. The two must be balanced, easy to cast and neither too heavy nor too light. Rods and reels are built for a category of fishing action to make the sport pleasurable and somewhat productive. You could use a surf rod for brook trout fishing but it's not much fun and you probably wouldn't catch anything. Consult a salesperson and experienced fish afficionados before you buy.

With modifications for size and scale, certain rod and reel combinations can be mixed. For example, surf rods are available with a surf spinning reel. This reel is identical in every respect to the standard spinning reel except it is much larger. In fact, spinning reels now come in a wide range of sizes, as do standard saltwater reels.

Selecting A Rod

Rod	Length	Material	Sections	Reel	Action	Notes	Area to use
Surf	7' to 14'	Tubular fiberglass	1 or 2	Spin or spool	Stiff	Large butt line guides	Saltwater beach
Fly	8' to 9'	Wood or tubular fiberglass	2 or 3	Fly	Very flexible	Weighs 4 to 5 ounces	Lake, stream, bay
Boat, Bay or Trolling	5' to 7'	Solid or tubular fiberglass	1 or 2	Salt-water	Stiffest	Avoid "spring" tips	Inshore, offshore
Bait-casting	5½' to 6'	Wood or tubular fiberglass	1	Bait	Flexible	Must feel good	Lakes, rivers, bays
Spinning	5' to 8'	Tubular fiberglass	1 or 2	Spin or spin-cast	Flexible and whippy	Light Large guide lines	Anywhere
Simplest	12' to 16'	Cane or bamboo	1	None	Very whippy	Simple pole	Creeks, ponds, streams, lakes

Leaders and Lines

Leaders connect the hook to the fishing line and serve two functions. They deceive the fish by separating the hook or lure from the more visible tackle such as sinkers, swivels and lines. Leaders also give added strength at the end of the rig, which is the area of greatest shock. Leaders meant to remain invisible to fish are usually made of monofilament; those meant to absorb shock or to be strong enough so that fish teeth cannot break them are usually made of wire. The type of leader you choose and the length varies with the fish you are seeking.

The first fishing lines were probably made from braided horse hair or twisted animal sinew. Today, lines are made of artificial, manufactured materials. They are sold in a broad variety of "pound tests" (number of pounds it takes to break the line). Fishing lines have a practical low of 4 to 6 pound test (fly fishing) to a practical high of approximately 150 pound test (big game fishing). The 15 to 40 pound test lines are the workhorses of most sport fishing.

The three principal materials used in making lines for sport fishing are dacron, nylon and monofilament. They may be braided or in single

21

strands. In special cases wire lines may be used. Monel is an expensive, durable but difficult line to use.

It's important to remember to get the proper balance or match between your rod, reel, and line. For example, a good spinning rod and reel on which you force 100 lb. test wire is a very unmatched combination. And, it would be foolish to put 6 lb. test monofilament on a stout boat rod and reel to fish for sharks.

Here are some general properties of various fishing lines:

Line Properties

Line type	Stretch	Abrasion resistance	Knot strength	Fishing versatility
Dacron	Minimal	Medium	Medium	Medium
Wire	None	High	Low	Low
Lead Core	None	High	Low	Low
Braided Nylon	Medium	Medium	Medium	Medium
Monofilament	High	Low	High	High
Fly Line	Medium	Medium	Medium	Low

Each type of line has its own uses, its own traits, and is available in a range of colors and strengths.

Monofilament is ideal for spinning reels but can be used on almost all reels. It comes in a wide range of pound tests, from 2 lbs. to 200 lbs. It is basically a single strand of extruded nylon.

Braided dacron is made of many strands of dacron with a hollow core. It's stiffer and less stretchy than braided nylon and is best on a boat rod. It's sometimes difficult to tie into knots, but it can be used in most conventional fishing situations.

Braided nylon is excellent for bait casting and big game fishing.

Fly line is made just for fly rods. It can be tapered or plastic-coated, and have different sinking rates, or float. Fortunately, fly rods are usually marked with the proper line size to use, since the classifications are confusing to the novice.

Wire and *lead core lines* are used to fish in deep waters or for trolling.

Smaller-sized lines mean further casting, minimum visibility, and maximum line storage on reel. A large spool is usually your best buy.

But remember that smaller lines are not meant for big game fishing. Here are some line care tips:

- Avoid continuous contact with the sun.
- Avoid contact with "chemicals," such as gas, oil, suntan lotion, or insect repellent.
- Always check for abrasion and wear before a trip.
- Keep your reel spool full.
- Clean your line with fresh water and special line cleaners after use.

Rigs

A rig is the catching arrangement of line, lure, hook, swivel, leader, sinker and bait used in the water. Sophisticates like to call this *terminal tackle.*

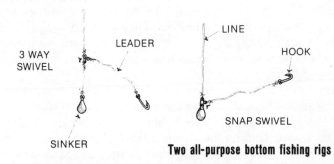

Two all-purpose bottom fishing rigs

You can get by with only two bottom fishing rigs for bait fishing. The one on the right lends itself well to the small to medium-sized fresh and saltwater spinning rod and reel. A terminal snap swivel can hold both the sinker and the loop of the leader. The rig on the left is most suited to boat, casting and surf rods.

Use the rig on the right to fish with an artificial lure. Simply remove the sinker and hook, tie an appropriate "snap swivel" to the end of the monofilament line, and snap on the artificial bait of your choice. Use a clinch knot to tie the swivel to the line.

Lures

A lure is an artificial bait that comes in all sizes, shapes, colors and materials and is used in fresh and saltwater fishing. It looks like food to the fish but is not edible. Sometimes a lure attracts fish by angering them or forcing them to be defensive. For example, some freshwater panfish, like bluegills, build spawning beds and if you cast nearby repeatedly, the fish may bite in irritation. Some lures have no hooks. They serve only to attract the fish, which is actually caught by using another rod with another kind of hooked bait. Attracting lures are called "teasers."

Again, you'll want to match your lure to the fish you are after, to the body of water where you are fishing (the terrain) and to your tackle. Let's take a brief look at some lure types.

Jigs are below-surface lures ("the jig is down") that incorporate a lead head, hook and eye for tying leader or line. The hook shaft is variously decorated with bristles, hairs, feathers, rubber or plastic strands. Jigs are excellent for catching small saltwater fish or freshwater fish of any size and are most adaptable to spinning tackle.

Spoons are flattened, generally oval metal pieces with complex curves of various colors and finishes. They are used in casting and trolling for many saltwater fish, including mackerel, sea trout, snook, baracuda, jack, bluefish and some freshwater varieties, such as trout, bass and pike.

Spinners are lighter weight metal blades that revolve or spin around a central shaft. This lure incorporates the spinning effect attached to a more conventional jig, and is available in various weights, and with different hooks, feathers and beads attached. Spinners are widely used in freshwater fishing to catch panfish, bass, pike and muskies, but are rarely used in any kind of saltwater fishing.

Plugs are elongated, full-bodied lures made of wood or plastic and resemble a minnow, baitfish, frog or crayfish. They generally have at least two sets of treble hooks (three hooks in one unit) and come in a variety of sizes and colors. They also have different actions. Some sink, some float, some dart, some jerk, some dive, some move straight, some move in midwater column. Plugs are used for casting or trolling, most commonly when fishing for freshwater bass. Using plugs requires experience and experimentation—and you can't get one without the other, so go ahead and try 'em, beginners.

Flies are freshwater trout catcher's Nirvana. However, they are being found increasingly in the saltwater fishing tackle box as well, by anglers going after tarpon, mackerel, baracuda, dolphin, and bonefish. Coming in various materials and colors, flies can be surface floaters ("dry") or sinkers ("wet"), and are ideally matched with the fly rod and reel.

A final category of lures is relatively new, and may soon disappear as oil reserves deplete. The so-called "plastics" are replicas of various baits—worms, frogs, squids, minnows, crayfish, shrimp—and come in numerous colors and sizes. They are most popular for freshwater fishing but they are being used more and more in the bay too, especially for sea trout, drum and croaker. They usually come unrigged without a hook.

Sinkers

Sinkers have two basic shapes: rounded or square edged. Round sinkers include the ball and the egg. Square-edge sinkers include the diamond and pyramid.

The water's bottom and the type of fish you are seeking will partially determine which sinker is most appropriate. Stiff currents, surf conditions, depth of water, tide and tackle type will also affect your choice.

Round sinkers are for rock bottoms or fishing on sunken obstructions and debris. Square-edge sinkers are used in sand and mud bottoms.

Egg sinkers have a hole through the center for threading your line, so they are free to slip along your line. Shaped like an egg, they are used for trolling or fast drifting when you are trying to keep your bait deep, usually in saltwater fishing.

The lightest sinkers, such as split-shots, clinchers and rubbercores are used to add small amounts of casting weight, or to get the sinker just a little bit deeper, usually in freshwater fishing.

You should always carry a good assortment of all sizes and shapes to meet various fishing conditions.

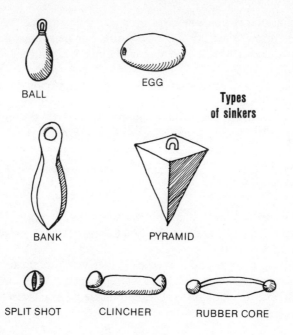

BALL

EGG

Types
of sinkers

BANK

PYRAMID

SPLIT SHOT

CLINCHER

RUBBER CORE

Hooks

Hooks come in a variety of subtle shapes and not-so-subtle sizes. There are perhaps 20 different hook designs. The hook size you use is determined by the size of fish you are after; the hook shape or pattern is determined by the species you are after.

The claw or beak hook is popular for general bottom fishing but the O'Shaughnessy is flattened for strength and catches the big ones off the bottom. The Sproat hook is a good all-around freshwater hook for big fish. The Carlisle and Chestertown hook patterns are long shanked and catch flounder, fluke and eels. They are easy to remove from a fish's mouth. Whatever your fishing interest, there is a hook size and shape best suited for the job. Hooks made of stainless steel cost more, but hold their sharpness longer.

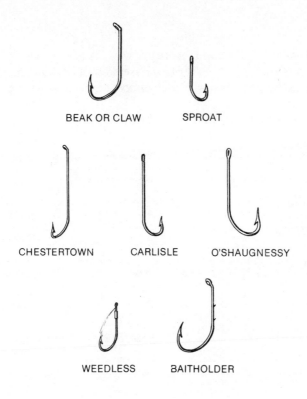

BEAK OR CLAW

SPROAT

CHESTERTOWN

CARLISLE

O'SHAUGNESSY

WEEDLESS

BAITHOLDER

We could devote an entire book to the subject of rigs used in trolling. Again, my advice is to get advice. Consult someone experienced with trolling. You will want to learn the techniques of trolling eventually since many game fish are caught in this way.

Reserve most of your rig decisions until you get to the tackle store. Look over what is available and talk to the sales clerk. Read some fish magazines. Try to identify the basic equipment we have discussed here. Buy these first and learn to use them to catch fish. Get fancy, expensive things later, if you decide you need them.

Bait

Bait can be used in a wide variety of ways. A type of fish may scorn its known favorite bait and strike a lesser known bait of poor quality. Sometimes, a given fish will "hit" almost anything you throw in the water.

Here are a few general tips for bait use:

Major bait types	How to rig	Where to fish	How to fish
Earthworms	⅓ on hook	Bottom or in water column	Stand still; use sinker or float
Marine worms	⅓ on hook	Saltwater bottom or in water column	Stand still; use sinker or float
Cut fish pieces	Hook strip 1 to 3 times on bare hook or lure	Bottom or in water column	Stand still; trolling, drifting, casting
Cut squid	Hook strip 1 to 3 times on bare hook or lure	Bottom or in water column	Stand still; trolling, drifting, casting
Live shrimp	Hook through front of head or arch of tail, avoid black spot in head	Bottom, usually shallow areas or water column	No sinker; allow shrimp to roam and swim
Live minnows	Hook through mouth or back below dorsal fin	Bottom, usually shallow areas of water water column	No sinker; allow shrimp to roam and swim
Crabs	Hook through top and bottom shell, offset to side	Bottom	Stand still; use sinker
Eels and whole fish	Multiple hooks and thread with stiff wire	Usually saltwater column	Trolling, casting, drifting
Mealworms	Thread through hook	Freshwater	Casting with splitshot
Live sand fleas	Hook through shell but avoid vital organs	Bottom in saltwater beaches	Light sinker, surf casting or pier
Crayfish	Hook through carapace or tail	Bottom in freshwater or estuaries	Very light sinker, bait or spincasting
Crickets	Through back	Freshwater column	Drifting or from shore with cane pole
Pork rinds	Hook once on artificial lure	Usually freshwater column	Trolling or casting

Keeping bait alive

Catalpa worms are the larvae of the catalpa sphinx moth. They ordinarily die a few hours after being taken from their food trees but by placing a jar of catalpa worms in the refrigerator, you can keep them alive for one or two days.

Crickets can be kept in a perforated container in a dry, warm and ventilated area. A supply of corn meal will serve as food. Pack moist cotton into the top of the container when you leave on a fishing trip.

Keep earthworms in a perforated container filled with rich soil or bedding. Place moist peat moss over the top.

Mealworms are kept in wheat germ, bran, cornmeal, etc. Refrigerate them to prevent the larvae from maturing to beetles.

Crayfish stay fresh when kept in running stream water. Feed them small amounts of ground meat. They can be transported on ice.

Minnows and shrimp are easily kept alive in live bait wells built into boats. Live bait buckets are also serviceable. Keep them away from direct sunlight; too much heat will kill them both. Keep the water fresh and clean.

Sand fleas can be kept in wet sand; and blood worms should be kept in the shade under moist seaweed.

Dead baits, usually purchased frozen, need to be thawed but not in direct sunlight. Cut into pieces or kept whole, they can be used for fishing the bottom, for drifting or rigged for trolling and casting.

Rod and Reel Fishing—Casting Types

The secret to rod and reel fishing is learning to cast, and no special talents are required. Timing, coordination and form are the ingredients and with a bit of practice, you'll develop these. Perfection is not necessary. All casts break down to steps. Drill yourself on the different steps, then practice the whole cast.

Good casting permits you to place your bait where you want it, and saves you endless frustration unsnarling your line or straightening backlashes. You'll be spending more time with your bait in the water. Combine this skill with well-stocked waters and good knowledge of your gear, and you'll go home with a full stringer of fish.

The casting techniques vary with the type of rod and reel used. Let's look at the rod and reel casting types.

Bait casting

Bait casting is used almost exclusively for freshwater fishing. With With the reel spool facing up, or more accurately, slightly to the left, with your right thumb on the spool, hold the rod in front of you at the two o'clock position. Your upper arm extends outward away from your hip, and your forearm is almost parallel to the ground and in line with the rod. The bait should dangle 2″ to 8″ from the rod tip.

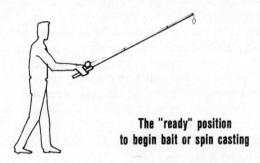

**The "ready" position
to begin bait or spin casting**

Bring the rod up sharply so it is nearly vertical.

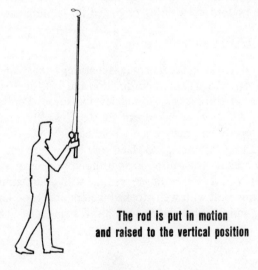

**The rod is put in motion
and raised to the vertical position**

As the bait snaps backward from the motion, it will flex the rod backward. At the same time, cock your wrist back.

Momentum flexes rod back accompanied by cocking the wrist backward

At this instant, snap the rod forward in the direction you wish to cast, releasing your forearm and wrist. Release your thumb when the rod is at the one o'clock position. Hold your thumb lightly on the spool so it can still turn, but never remove your thumb entirely to avoid backlash. You may also use your thumb as a brake to avoid overcasting your target.

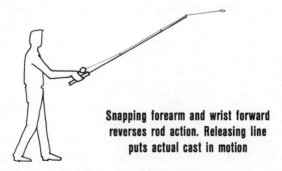

Snapping forearm and wrist forward reverses rod action. Releasing line puts actual cast in motion

Just before the bait reaches its target position, apply firm pressure on the spool with your thumb. Bring the rod to the two o'clock position as a follow-through.

31

Spin casting

The spinning rod and reel is perhaps the most versatile and easy to master of all the rod and reel combinations. Beginners would do well to use it first.

The movements and positions of casting with a spinning rod are almost identical to bait casting. The main difference is that the spinning reel is attached to the underside of the rod, facing the ground. Thus, your wrist is not turned, as in bait casting. "Shake hands" with a spinning rod. Your forefinger is looped around under the line and serves a function similar to the thumb in bait casting. Release the line as the tip of the rod points to the target. To stop the bait on target, simply turn the reel handle until the bail closes.

The *spinning side cast* is done when you are covered with overhanging trees and can't do the overhead cast. Simply stand erect, point the rod toward the target, with your forearm parallel to the ground and your wrist pointing upward. Flex your wrist so the rod whips ninety degrees, now pointing to your right, and whipping back. Flex your wrist back again so the rod snaps back toward target as you release the line from your forefinger.

You can picture the right-handed spinning side cast another way. Imagine a clock on the ground with you in its center. Orient the clock so the target is at the 11 o'clock position. Now you face 12 o'clock. This will leave the target slightly to your left but ahead. Point the rod toward one o'clock and flex your wrist back so the rod whips back to the three or four o'clock position. At this point, return your wrist with snapping motion and release the line at 12 o'clock. The momentum of the whipping rod will carry the bait forward to land at the 11 o'clock position, which is the position of your target.

Surf and fly casting

Surf and fly casting are somewhat more specialized techniques. They are also the most difficult casts to learn and master. Surf casting is used exclusively for saltwater beach fishing. The cast is done with a long rod, using a full whipping action created by twisting and exerting the body. It is a vigorous cast requiring strength and power. As much as six ounces of lead may be used in the surf rig.

Fly casting is for open lake, stream and river fishing and represents the other extreme in casting. Fly casting requires a light touch, finesse and economy of motion. Maximum hand/eye coordination are needed. Great reliance is placed on the wrist, forearm and elbow.

To learn these casting methods, consult the bibliography. Or better yet, find someone experienced in these casting methods to offer you some personal instruction.

Bay casting

Bay or boat rods resemble heavy, bulky bait-casting rigs and are not really for accurate or distance casting. They are generally used to lower baits to the water's bottom in bays or shallow water offshore, when it is necessary to get clear of a boat, pier or rocks. Boat rigs are generally used only for saltwater fishing from a boat, although some people use them for trolling, drift fishing or fishing from piers and jetties. Only short, relatively inaccurate casts are possible, so it is best used only to get clear of a boat, pier or rocks.

A modern offshoot of the boat rod is the trolling rod, which comes in a variety of sizes and strengths. No casting is done with it. Simply pay out line to a distance that depends on the fish you seek, while the boat is moving. The bait is towed or trolled. This relatively modern embellishment is practiced extensively by commercial charter boat fleets from California to New England.

Knots

All rod and reel fishing can be done using only two knots: the clinch knot and the square knot. The clinch knot is secure and strong and is used to tie line or leader to any hook, sinker, snap swivel or other line. It is tied by placing the free or tag end through the eye and twisting it around the main part at least six times. Then, pull the free end back through the first loop created by the twists and pull it tight.

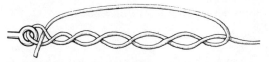

The clinch knot connects anything for fishing readiness

The improved *clinch knot* is made by coming back through the big loop (created by the free end) *after* passing through the first loop. In either case, make sure that upon tightening, the coils are in a spiral and not overlapping. Remember that two clinch knots, one from each piece, will connect two lines or leaders.

The *square knot* is the simplest of all the knots. The only variation you will use is that the free end will be a loop.

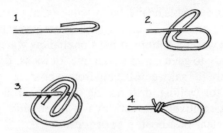

A square knot with a loop to create a loop

This is a good knot for creating a loop on the free end of leader or line.

A few other knots are useful to meet all your fishing needs. In the following drawings, one drawn line represents a fishing line.

The *palomar knot* ties a line or leader to a hook or swivel. Double over the end of the leader for about 10″ to create a loop (or two lines).

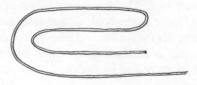

Place the loop through the eye of a hook, swivel, etc.

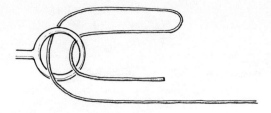

Now tie a square knot but don't tighten it.

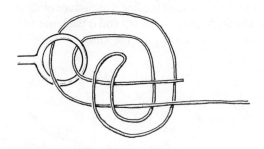

Finally, slip the loop end over the hook or swivel before tightening.

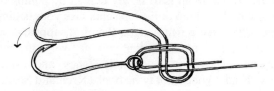

The palomar knot

Here's a knot for looping the end of a leader that's trickier than the simple square knot, but will result in a strong, secure loop. It can also be used to secure a hook or swivel.

Loop the end of the line to create a circle about the size of a half dollar piece.

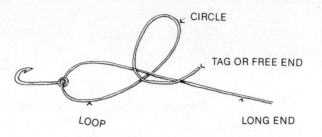

CIRCLE

TAG OR FREE END

LOOP

LONG END

Now wind the tag end of the line a minimum of three times through the circle and the long end. The tag end is the loose end or the working end that you use to actually tie the knot.

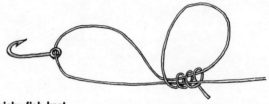

A tricky fish knot

Now the critical point is to slowly tighten by pulling *only the tag end.* Do not pull the loop or the long end. Use your fishing pliers. As you tighten, you see a figure eight, then it disappears.

There are some other knots that you may wish, in time, to add to your arsenal. They are good knots, fancy and useful, but not necessary. Find a good knot tying book (Kreh and Sosin's, noted in the reference section, is excellent) and learn:

- Jansik special: A very strong knot used in big game freshwater fishing.
- Blood knot: Used to connect two lines of similar diameter; common in saltwater offshore fishing.
- Surgeon's knot: Used to connect two lines of very unequal diameter; very common in freshwater fly fishing.
- Bimini twist: Makes a "double leader" giving more strength and shock absorbing capability for offshore big game saltwater trolling.

36

Vic Dunaway, a well-known fishing author, editor, and fish master, invented a knot tying system called the uni-knot system that can meet every saltwater and freshwater fishing need if you learn just one basic knot.

The uni-knot represents one basic tying operation. It is called a "system" because it can be used for almost all of the basic fishing knot needs, such as joining two lines, tying a line to terminal tackle, connecting leaders to line, attaching line to a reel spool, snelling a hook and even making shock leaders and double lines.

Basically the knot is tied as follows:

Pass a line through a line loop, lure, swivel, eye of hook, etc. In the above example a hook eye is attached to a leader. Run it through about 6″ to 8″, making the lines parallel, and then bring the tag end back toward the connection point to form a circle. As in the second drawing, make about six turns with the tag end through the circle (around the double line). Pull the tag tightly to close up the turns. The result should approximate the third drawing. Finally, pull the standing line so the loop closes and the knot slides up against the connection point, the eye of a hook in this case. Now pull both ends again to make it tight. Needle nose pliers are very helpful in making this system work for you. Finally, trim off the tag end, leaving a very short stub.

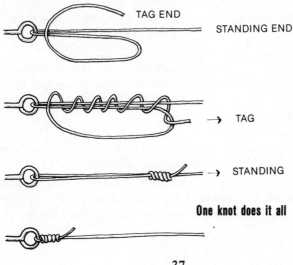

TAG END

STANDING END

→ TAG

→ STANDING

One knot does it all

All knots and knot systems described here perform at above ninety percent (and most at ninety-five percent) efficiency. Obviously all knots represent a weak point in the system, but these knots are at least ninety percent as strong as the unbroken, uncut, untied line itself.

Fishing Extras

Like everything else, tackle boxes come in a variety of sizes and materials. Commonly a rectangular plastic box, your best bet opens from the top and has a fold-out trunk, with at least two trays. What do you put in the tackle box? Everything but your rod, reel, bait, clothing and edibles! There are also specialty boxes, i.e., fly box or plastic lure box, but don't buy these until you become a specialist.

You must not only hook and battle a fish but also land it. There are two main types of landing gear: nets and gaffs. A freshwater wading net has a small hoop and a short handle with an elongated net bag and an elastic cord on the handle. The cord is tied to the angler and allowed to hang free. A boat net intended for larger fish has a hoop of wider diameter with a long handle and a grip. Gaffs are large, strong hooks fixed to a handle 2′ to 5′ long. They are used in saltwater fishing.

Netting and gaffing takes some practice. Here is the shortest landing course you can take:

Netting: Put your net in the water before the fish is close by; as the fish draws closer, put the net deeper into the water and when the fish is next to you, place your net under it and lift up the fish.

Gaffing: When the fish is alongside you, place the gaff deep into the water, keeping the handle close to the fish without touching it, then lift evenly and quickly so the hook strikes the belly or head area. Continue lifting, following through.

Other landing gear includes guns (needed only for very large sharks) and billy clubs. Clubs can stun a biting fish, such as a baracuda or shark, before you put it in the boat.

Caught fish must be stored properly to retain fish meat quality. Most small boaters today use plastic or styrofoam coolers with a layer of ice on bottom. Large boats have fish boxes for holding the larger fish generally caught in offshore waters. Freshwater wading purists use a basket attached to the hip, called a creel. Stringers are popular when fishing from the shore, a bank or in very small boats.

If you will be fishing from a boat, a few other accessories are helpful. Depth recorders will give an index to bottom terrain. Outriggers are long poles that extend from the sides of a boat. By attaching the fishing line from the rod to the outrigger tip one can fish by trolling several lines, keeping them separate.Downriggers are special devices that aid in trolling several baits very deep. They are common in the Great Lakes, where they are used for deepwater trout. Both are trolling aids used on boats. Trolling motors propel a small boat at a slow trolling speed, and if you are fishing for freshwater bass, they are now regarded as indispensable. To be really fancy, assuming you know something about fish ecology, you can use depth thermometers.

Tools can be invaluable on a trip. Here is a list of helpful items:
- Pliers (needlenose and "fishermen's")
- Nail clippers
- Hook remover and scaler
- Pocket knife with multiple accessories
- Several small screwdrivers
- Waterproof glue or heavy tape

These tools are for fishing needs. Don't omit tools you need for emergency boat or motor repair. At the same time do not carry cumbersome non-essentials. Sharpening stones, for example, are nnecessary—your knives and hooks should be sharpened *before* the fishing trip.

Footwear is important on a fishing trip. On boats, no-slip shoes or rubber boots are helpful. For saltwater surf or freshwater wading, hip boots or waders are invaluable. On cold days, insulated waterproof boots can make or break the trip.

There are also some cases and holders available to protect your expensive gear. There are manufactured cases for your rods and reels, but as your interest and equipment grow, you might want to design your own to suit your own needs. Rod mounts on a boat are handy because in choppy water they protect rods from being broken.

There are numerous devices for holding specific types of bait: buckets, traps, cages, bottles, boxes, etc. There are even pocket air pumps to keep holding water well oxygenated. More of this in the next section.

Saltwater and Freshwater Fishing

Fishing in fresh water is not very different from saltwater fishing. The two share basic similarities, which must be learned, practiced, mastered and then practiced some more—whether you are a beginner or fish master.

There are a few general differences, however. Freshwater fishing is usually more closely regulated. You'll need more information about bag limits, size minima, seasons, licenses, etc. for fresh fishing. Tackle shops or local offices of your state fish or natural resources agency can usually tell you everything you need to know. Freshwater fishing usually is more specialized since you are ordinarily seeking one specific type of fish, and it generally involves lighter gear. Freshwater fishing is easier on your equipment.

In either case, practice safety on your trips. Bring along a first aid kit. Learn all regulations. Respect the environment: Keep it clean; be a user, not an abuser. Approach all water with caution—it's not *your* environment—you are a terrestrial organism!

A list of tips:

- Never go alone.
- Don't hop on rocks, mounds of grass or mud.
- Always wear shoes.
- Don't stay out in storms.
- Don't get drunk or drugged.
- Follow common sense boat behavior.
- Pay attention to your surroundings, watching the weather, water, and possible shore obstructions.
- Be considerate to fishing comrades.

A word on removing hooks from the body. If the hook is deeply embedded anywhere or superficially embedded in vital areas such as an eye, the tongue, along the spinal cord, in the palm of the hand, in the belly region or the groin, do not attempt to remove it. Cut the line and protect area from further injury, then go to a physician.

For superficial problems in less critical areas, such as the forearm, finger, or toe, you can gently manipulate the hook with a pliers. remember the barb—you must first push the hook in before pulling it out because the barb points in the opposite direction from the point of the hook. Examine a bare hook to better understand its anatomy.

I advise taking a course in first aid through a local, competent organization. Help is usually difficult to find on a fishing trip.

Make Your Own

There are numerous books available on the subject of rodmaking, reel repair, fly, lure, and plug making. All the parts, tools, materials and accessories you need can be purchased. There are clubs in which members make their own tackle. Some have opened a small business in their homes. Others do it for a living. The main thing to understand is that if you want to make or repair your own fishing equipment, it is fairly simple to learn how.

The Final Word

Skill is an essential part of sports style fishing and this skill can be cultivated with experience and careful observation. But the principal ingredient is that intangible called luck.

Fish catching results aside, my advise is to simply enjoy fishing. It will relax you, bring you closer to nature and perhaps even closer to family or friends. Or even yourself!

Take it slow and enjoy whatever comes your way and fishing is guaranteed to add years to your life.

Catch only what you can use. Don't be greedy with nature or it will punish you . . . . and your children . . . . and their children . . . .

References

Angler's Guide to Saltwater Fishing in the Northeast. K. Wilcoxson. 1975. Herman Publishers. Boston, Massachusetts.

Modern Fresh and Salt Water Fly Fishing. C. Waterman. 1974. Macmillan. New York, New York.

How to Catch Fish in Saltwater. V. Evanoff. 1970. Fisherman's Information Bureau. Chicago, Illinois. (Simple, for the beginner.)

Practical Fishing Knots. L. Kreh and M. Sosin. 1975. 4th edition. Crown Publishers. New York, New York. (An authoritative, complete book on the subject.)

The Complete Guide to Salt and Fresh Water Fishing Equipment. B. Wisner. 1976. Doubleday. New York, New York.

How to Catch Salt-Water Fish. B. Wisner. 1973. Doubleday. New York, New York.

Saltwater Game Fishing. Joe Brooks. 1968. International Marine Publishing. Camden, Maine.

Surf Fishing. V. Evanoff. 1974. International Marine Publishing. Camden, Maine.

Successful Ocean Game Fishing. Frank Moss. 1971. International Marine Publishing. Camden, Maine.

Fisherman's Handbook. R. Allyn. Great Outdoors Publishing. St. Petersburg, Florida. (A very complete reference type book.)

Modern Saltwater Fishing Table. Frank Moss. 1977. International Marine Publishing. Camden, Maine.

Complete Book of Baits, Rigs and Tackle. Vic Dunaway. Wickstrom Publishing. Coral Gables, Florida.

A History of the Fish Hook. H. J. Hurum. 1978. Winchester Press. New York, New York. (Read for fun— very interesting!)

Fishing Fundamentals for Beginning Anglers. AFTMA Center. 1979. Arlington Heights, Illinois. (The best I've seen on the subject.

Murray's Fishing Guide: Maine to Florida Keys. Ken D. Murray. 1978. Murray Publishing. Wethersfield, CT.

Fishing the Texas Surf. Tony Fedler. 1978. Sea Grant Program, Texas A&M University. College, Texas. (A brief, helpful guide to surf, pier and wade fishing. Excellent for Gulf of Mexico sports fishing.)

Handbook of Knots and Splices. C. E. Gibson. 1963. Emerson Books. Buchanan, New York.

Fishing Rigs for Fresh and Salt Water. Vlad Evanoff. 1977. Harper and Row. New York, New York.

Fishing with Small Fry: A Parent's Guide to Teaching Children How to Fish. Jim Freeman. 1973. Chronicle Books. San Francisco, California.

Oldies but Goodies:

American Fisherman's Guide. Bill Bueno. Prentice-Hall Co. Englewood Cliffs, New Jersey.

The Fisherman's Encyclopedia. I. N. Gabrielson, ed. The Stackpole Co. Harrisburg, Pennsylvania.

The Complete Book of Fishing. Larry Koller. Bobbs-Merrill Co. Columbus, Ohio.

Fly Fishing. A. J. McClane. Prentice-Hall Co. Englewood Cliffs, New Jersey.

Spinning for Fresh and Salt Water Fish of North America. A. J. McClane. Prentice-Hall Co. Englewood Cliffs, New Jersey.

CHAPTER TWO
Survive!

Catching Fish for Profit

In the land of plenty there was never any need to discuss self-sufficiency and survival skills. Such knowledge was lost with the pioneers.

But Americans are canning their food again. They're making their own wine and doing their own repairs. They have gardens. They're calling themselves homesteaders, going back to the land to live off small acreages, and saying we must train ourselves to become self-sufficient. This chapter is devoted to that view because, like the homesteaders, I can see that there ain't plenty of anything in this land anymore.

Remember the goal of survival fishing is to catch fish to eat or sell. Unlike someone fishing for pleasure, the survivalist usually pursues a wide variety of fish types, sizes and quantities, and primarily uses mass-catching gear, which is often homemade.

Before I tell you how to fish for survival, again remember the basic survival rule: Catch only what you and your loved ones can eat or sell. Don't waste any of the earth's precious gift of food. If you question that rule, remember again why there is even a need to learn survival

43

methods. Consider why there ain't plenty.

To start: Fish live in water. Sounds trite, but you'll need to keep in mind that the task of fishing is much more difficult than any land-based activity. You seldom see your prey and you can't see their habitat. Might be easier to hunt eagles with a pea-shooter.

Some of these methods require a boat. One or two people with their own inexpensive work boat can catch enough to feed their own families all year long.

Not all the methods described here are legal in all states; many require a permit or license. Some involve neither and can be used in most places with little difficulty.

These methods work. That means if you do everything right, have the correct conditions with a little luck, and the fish are in the vicinity, you are going to catch one hell of a lot of fish. Be prepared, with some methods, for hundreds of pounds. Make sure you have freezer space and friends or family lined up for fish gifts, or a sales market. Gear up to can, freeze, smoke, brine and eat.

Be observant. Note the time and circumstances when you do well. Be mindful of tides, currents, seasons, sunlight, cloudiness of the water (turbidity), temperature, type of bait, time of day, etc.

Let's take a look at the simple methods first, and then we'll get fancy.

Entrapment

One of the most basic methods of survival fishing is to maneuver one or two unsuspecting fish into a corral of some kind. Native Americans used this method in mountain streams and it is still used commonly in many Pacific islands.

Use of the tides is probably the easiest technique. When the tide is high, wade out into the water and walk parallel to the shore, if possible. This will help drive some fish nearer the shore. Build a simple dam in a halfmoon shape, from sticks, rocks, dead corral or sediment, or anything else that makes an effective barrier. As the tide recedes and the water level falls below your barrier, you may have entrapped a few small fish.

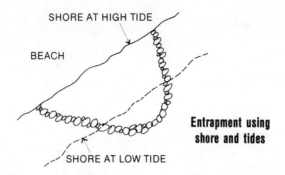

Entrapment using shore and tides

Or, in shallow freshwater streams, build an enclosed barrier out of rocks and sand, with a funnel-like opening facing downstream.

Walk upstream toward your barrier until you spot a fish. Then slowly and patiently maneuver the fish into your barrier. Don't lose sight of it. When the fish is driven through the opening, you can quickly seal it off with one or two rocks at the narrow part of the funnel. Extract the fish with a dipnet, your shirt, a burlap bag, your hands or a bucket.

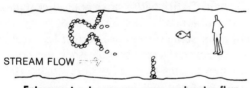

Entrapment using narrow space and water flow

Poke Pole Fishing

To rig a poke pole takes only a few materials and very little money. You need a flexible but sturdy pole 6′ to 12′ long. Bamboo poles are excellent. A variety of small hooks are helpful and you'll also need stainless steel wire and winding thread or tape. Add some bait and you're equipped to catch a meal of small panfish.

The poke pole rig should look like this:

Poke pole rig

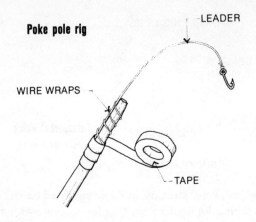

LEADER

WIRE WRAPS

TAPE

Note:
- The wire leader is less than 24".
- The leader is wrapped to the pole with more wire.
- Wrap the leader the final time with tightly wound thread or strong waterproof tape.

Use baits common to your area. Shrimp, squid, cut fish and mussels are always good bait. To fish with a poke pole, stick it into pools and crevices and under or around rocks. Tide pools, rocky shores at low tide, jetties and other similar areas are perfect for poke poling.

Do not stay in one spot. If a crevice, hole, rock, etc. doesn't produce in a few minutes, move along. Keep away from rough surf. Carry a fish stringer on your belt. Keep moving.

In a couple of hours your family will have a meal.

Stunning and Stupefying

Fish can be temporarily stunned, then captured in a variety of ways. Some of the techniques are crude; some are downright violent, dangerous and illegal.

One of the simplest and most acceptable is to locate a fish lingering just below a brittle, not-too-thick layer of clear ice. Simply beat heavily on the ice directly over the head of the fish with a club, mallet or hammer. Your goal is not to break through the ice to strike the fish, but to create crashing vibrations or shock waves to break up the top layers of ice. The fish will be momentarily stunned, giving you time to cut a hole in the ice, using a tool such as a claw hammer or pick, and retrieve it.

A more crude method is to locate a fish in shallow water and hit it with a stone or stick, aiming for the head. A lucky hit will stun the fish long enough for you to remove it from the water.

Explosives or electrical fields will also stupefy fish, but they are cruel and destructive. Don't use poisons either, because they harm the whole environment—including you.

Spearing

Fishing with a spear is probably the oldest fishing method known. It is estimated that such fishing was done 10,000 years ago. With the advent of skin diving, then SCUBA diving, which made possible sustained contact with the fish's environment, spear fishing has evolved, and continues to be popular in this modern age.

Perhaps the simplest method of spearing, and one known to the Romans and Greeks, is night time gigging of flounder. Floyd's article, "Commercial Flounder Gigging," noted in the reference section, describes flounder gigging in shallow, protected coast and inland water, and Warlen's "Night Stalking Flounder in the Ocean Surf" discusses how it's done in the ocean surf. You can gig flounder in water from a few inches to several feet in depth, in the surf or a protected bay.

Surf floundering

The two most important pieces of gear are the gig and the light. Gigs vary in design and cost. The most elaborate are multi-pronged with wood shafts. Shop around at tackle and fishing supply stores.

You can fashion a serviceable and cheap gig at home, by sharpening any steel or aluminum rod to a point. Concrete reinforcing rods are excellent. The rod should be 4' to 6' long and about ⅜" in diameter. Remember that it must be heavy enough to withstand a 10 to 15 lb. fish, but light enough to handle while wading in the surf.

Some people like to adorn the surf gig with accessories. By placing the fish stringer line at the end opposite the sharpened point, for

47

example, you create a "flow-through automatic fish stringer."

Surf floundering is best done at night, by wading in water no deeper than up to your waist. You'll be carrying an underwater light, a spear and a fish stringer, and wearing waders. Wade slowly, guided by your light. When you spot a flounder, slowly position your spear over it. With a quick thrust, spear the fish, aiming at its head, preferably behind the gills. When the fish is not struggling violently, you can lift it from the water.

Usually the best season for surf floundering is autumn, when fish are moving from the chilly bays to the warmer surf.

Three other important environmental factors—surf zone, wind, and moon phase—affect your success. Scientists break the surf zone down to as many as four or five sections, but for our purposes, there are three basic zones. The intertidal sloping area is exposed at low tide; a trough of water runs parallel to the shoreline; and a bar separates the water trough from the ocean proper. The best floundering occurs from two hours before low tide to two hours after, on the bar or its outer edge. The trough is the next best. If there is no identifiable trough or bar, then you will do best by wading just beyond the breakers. Do not wade and spear in rip currents—such fast-moving seaward flows are dangerous and they hold few flounders.

Little or no wind is important. Waves, ripples, spray, etc. impair visibility and increase the hazards. Also, remember that several days of onshore wind (wind moving from sea to land) causes poor visibility by suspending sediment and debris. Wait for a few days of calm weather when the material settles.

The less moonlight the better. New moons and cloudy nights are generally more productive, since bright moonlight makes the fish more alert.

Warlen describes a very effective light for surf floundering. Since a picture is worth a thousand words . . . .

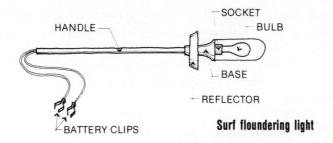

SOCKET
BULB
HANDLE
BASE
REFLECTOR
BATTERY CLIPS

Surf floundering light

The handle is ¾" PVC pipe, 4' to 6' long. One end is threaded to accommodate the reflector and base. All seams and joints are sealed with silicone rubber or with another caulking compound. The six to 12 volt battery can be worn as a shoulder or backpack.

Two final notes of caution: Don't confuse large stingrays for large flounders. Both are edible, but the stingray has a whip-like tail with a stinging barb.

And keep an eye out for sharks if you are wading in the surf at night.

Inshore floundering

Inshore flounder gigging is also best done on dark nights, when the weather is clear and still. If there is a bright moon, move toward it as you work your boat. Work against the current and fish on an outgoing tide, trying various depths.

The gigging light can be purchased commercially but any light that shows the ocean bottom—a good flashlight, or a battery, gasoline or oil-operated lantern with reflectors—can also be used.

The oldest light source is the wood fire. The gigging light is mounted on the bow of your boat and the fire is maintained in the mesh basket.

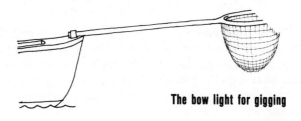

The bow light for gigging

49

If you want to build your own light, you can cut costs by 50 %. To be sure your design meets your needs, closely inspect the commercial models.

Also remember that inshore bay gigging can be done during the day. This simplifies your equipment needs: a gig, bathing suit, and a cooler on the shore. While usually not as productive, daytime gigging can be more fun, and you're likely to catch at least some stingrays, skates and flatfishes. Be prepared to thrust your gig sooner and further from your target than you would at night.

Underwater spearing

A variety of spears will work in underwater spear fishing. Some resemble the gigs previously described—a simple rod with a sharpened point or with the more sophisticated multi-pronged heads.

In addition to the hand-propelled spears, there are spears that are mechanically propelled. Elaborate and expensive guns are available commercially, but they are efficient, effective and dangerous.

In my opinion, the best is the simplest and cheapest. It is called the Hawaiian Sling and has been used in the Pacific for several centuries. I learned with a sling in the Florida Keys and sustained myself on the fish that I speared.

The sling is made of a wooden or aluminum tube, two sturdy strips, a metal cup and the spear, and is operated with one hand.

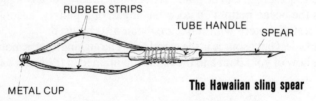

RUBBER STRIPS

TUBE HANDLE   SPEAR

METAL CUP   **The Hawaiian sling spear**

The metal cup resembles a sewing thimble. Place one end of the spear in the cup, then force the tube forward toward the spear point, stretching the rubber slings. Keep the stretch, with one hand holding both the tube and the spear. Aim with this hand and shoot by releasing your grip on the spear, keeping your grip on the tube. It is important to follow through—keep a steady, straight aim as the spear leaves the tube.

50

Needless to say, before you can master spearing techniques, you must learn to snorkel or SCUBA dive, and must feel at home in the water away from your boat. Get help from somebody who knows how and never dive alone, even after you think you've mastered the sport.

Line Fishing Without a Hooking Device

An entangling bob is made of anything that will entrap and tangle the fish's teeth momentarily. The bob will not hold the fish indefinitely, as a hook does, so the fish must be lifted quickly before it is aware of what is happening.

The entangling bob should be about the size of a softball or smaller. It is secured to a strong line, from 3' to 8' long. You can soak the bob in a bucket in which you have chopped up some baitfish, sea urchins, fish guts, etc., or bait it with fish or meat pieces or intertwined with worms.

You can make the bob from weaved twine, light wire, monofilament line or Luffa gourds. Weave and lace the material you choose into a gnarled, snarled mass. Then, weight the bob with a lead sinker, rock or whatever is available and tie the line to a stiff pole. Lower the bob to the water's bottom, slowly raise it one foot, then lower it again. Continue moving your bob up and down until you feel the tug of your catch, then lift the bob quickly in one motion onto your boat or the beach.

Of course, the fish can eventually let go or wiggle off. But with practice you can become quite proficient at bobbing.

Another hookless rig is the gorge. It was probably invented to overcome the obvious weakness of the bob. The gorge is nothing more than a single or double pointed short wooden stick or piece of steel or bone and it's great if you want to catch a large meat fish, such as a shark. You can fish from a boat, pier, jetty or beach.

While gorges seem to work best for large fish, you can vary the length of the gorge for different fish types. To catch fish under one foot use a gorge under one inch; for one to two feet long fish use a gorge up to approximately three inches. A six inch gorge will catch the BIG ones.

Some examples are pictured below.

51

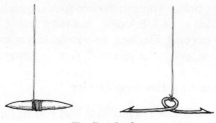

The first hook

Tie the line to the middle of the gorge, just off center to create two uneven lengths, i.e. a short and long end. Use a strong but lightweight line, and anchor the free end of the line to a tree or post.

Pierce the bait with the short end of the gorge first. The gorge should be parallel to the line.

Continue the insertion until the bait is skewered. You must permit the fish to swallow the baited gorge. When you pull on the line, the gorge becomes perpendicular to the line, as pictured above, and implants itself into the fish's belly or throat.

Be prepared to wait and then, if a large fish bites, be prepared for the struggle of your life.

The Handline

Using a handline is an old and simple method of fishing. The materials you need: A sturdy line, preferably nylon or dacron, a lead weight, 3-way swivels, some hooks, leader and bait. You may fish one or many hooks. Use fresh cut bait such as squid, fish, worms and shellfish.

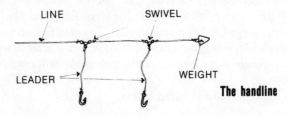

The handline

52

With a few hooks, you can throw the handline from a jetty, pier, rocks, etc. The leaders should be about 12" long with 14" to 16" between swivels. If you attach many hooks, you will need a small boat.

Bait your hooks, which should be attached to leaders.

You should have approximately 100 yards of line, weighted from eight ounces to three pounds, and it should be coiled neatly in a bucket until you are ready to use it. Dangle the weight on the end of the line over the side, and gradually pay out your line, tying or snapping a leader with the baited hook to each swivel on the line. When you reach the end, tie the line off on a cleat. Connect a floating marker buoy on a separate line every 20 to 30 yards. Then set back and relax awhile. If the fish are numerous you won't need to wait more than 30 minutes. If the action is slow, keep it in up to two hours. When you are ready to retrieve your line, neatly coil it back in the bucket. Wear gloves.

Experiment! Wait different lengths of time. Fish with different baits in different spots. Vary the size of your hook and the distance between hooks. An overly large fish can bite through or break a light leader. If you don't use a light leader, very large fish will destroy your handline. Because it will not be able to break off and escape, an overly large fish will destroy your rig with its fighting. Should a large fish snag or sever the handline, the periodic buoys will allow you to recapture at least part of your rig.

Ice Fishing

The cheapest and simplest ice fishing arrangement is simply a handline lowered through a hole in the ice. Use a heavy line, with from one to three baited hooks and a sinker. Large catches are possible with very low-cost equipment. Much of the gear you can make yourself or scrounge.

Ice fishing requires a few special pieces of equipment. First, you'll need to transport a blanket, tackle, lantern, equipment, knife, gloves and perhaps food and drink—maybe a thermos of hot coffee. Burlap bags have many uses when you're ice fishing.

What better implement to cart your equipment with than an old-fashioned sled. Since we are talking about survival techniques, let's not even consider snowmobiles. Fasten a wooden box on the sled that can serve as a carrier and seat while you're fishing. Design it so a lantern will fit under your chair to keep you warm.

To dig a hole in the ice, you'll need two tools: a chisel and a skimmer. You can make the chisel from a pipe ½" to 1" in diameter and about 5' long. Crimp one end of the pipe. A skimmer can be made by attaching with screws, nails and glue a wood shaft handle to a metal disc about 8" to 12" in diameter. Drill small holes in the disc and use the skimmer as a shovel to remove floating pieces of ice.

The Indians used "tip-ups" to aid in ice fishing, and you would do well to duplicate these first Americans. There are many variations but the basic tip-up principle is still used: Hook a fish and the flag will wave. With this simple implement you can handle several holes at once.

Tip-up for ice fishing

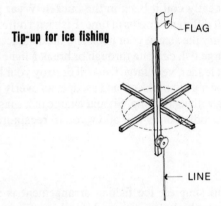

FLAG

LINE

Shanties are small, crude, makeshift houses carried directly onto the ice. People fish inside them! Shanties are popular among those who don't really enjoy ice fishing but who like eating and drinking outdoors on ice.

Bow and Arrow Fishing

If you are going to try bow and arrow fishing, use a bow that delivers an arrow accurately and powerfully. Carry a small file to keep a point on your arrow heads. Bow reels are available commercially. Wade slowly and wear Polaroid sunglasses.

Here's a tricky fact that may improve your accuracy. When you're out of the water, looking at an object in the water, the image you see is offset from the actual location. In short, your fish is not where it appears to be. The explanation of this confusing event is that air and water are different media and have different physical properties. Light rays are reflected from the fish and, as they pass out of the water on their way to your eyes, the rays bend. The rays speed up in air!

You must compensate for this in your aim. In general you must aim low or below the fish. Aim low, about two degrees below the fish when it is about 10' from you. As the distance between you and the fish increases beyond 10', gradually decrease your undershoot. At 20' to 25', aim directly at the fish without compensating for the distortion. When the fish is beyond 25' to 30' it is beyond your range.

Try bow and arrow fishing in the spring, when you're going after carp. Several excellent articles on this subject have appeared in a magazine called *Archery World,* available in most libraries.

Rippers

Some fish will strike at shiny unbaited hooks. Others travel in such dense schools that bait becomes unnecessary. Cod, perch, tuna, flatfish, bluefish, jacks and sturgeon can sometimes be caught with rippers.

Ripper rigs are simply a dense series of sharp hooks set in some pattern. The pattern can be a line or in a netlike set. They may be suspended from floats or set on the bottom. You might want to handline the rippers or set them on a short, stout pole. The catching principle is simple: Hooks and fish are so dense that the fish become entangled and pierced by the hooks.

This is an old and difficult method that takes some time to master. and I don't think it's worth the bother. For the slight additional expense and effort to obtain bait, you will enhance your chances by fishing the handline or some other baited hook rig.

Longlines

These rigs are similar to handline, but as the name implies, they are long. Up to 20 miles long in some cases! There are both horizontal and vertical longlines; horizontal longlines can be floating or bottom types.

The rigs are pictured below. In the fishing jargon; the line is called the longline, the leader a gangeon, and the weights are the leads.

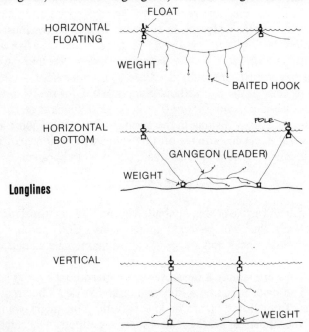

The longlines can be as long as you wish. These rigs are expensive, require more auxiliary equipment, and demand a large boat. You will certainly catch enough to eat with longlines, but given the expense, time and equipment necessary, don't count on enough fish to make a living this way. Professional longliners do make a living at it but they have invested a lot of time and money acquiring experience and equipment. The beginner would do well to keep the longline very short!

56

Snares, Traps and Pots

We are now entering the realm of the ideal for homesteaders and survivalists. Snares, traps and pots are reasonable in cost and easy to build, once you have tried a few. You can set as many as you need—from one to one thousand. Boat requirements and supporting equipment needs are minimal compared to other harvest gear. They are also simple to set and retrieve. There is one major drawback: You must know the behavior, habitat and food requirements of the critter you're after.

It has been my experience that commercial fishing crews who use traps and pots for a living know far more about the basic biology of the animals they seek than most academically trained biologists. Having worked closely with commercial crews and also being a trained biologist, I say this on fairly sound experience but add that both have something to offer. Sound biological information is valuable and a trained biologist is the best source of such advice.

If you can get guidance from an experienced trapper, you will be starting off right. Be prepared to do a lot of experimenting. Start by reading everything you can about the basic biology of the fish you want, and how to build and set traps. If you are an absolute beginner you will first need to find out which fish are in your area and which are trappable. I also recommend that you make an appointment with a local biologist to talk about which fish to seek. Look for experts at a local community college, university, laboratory, marine extension service or an environmental agency. Have a similar talk with a few locals. Check on applicable state or local laws.

Snares

Snares are probably the simplest in appearance but the most difficult to operate. Often they do not seem to work well, perhaps because using snares requires skill and patiences, traits many of us have lost. Only in so-called underdeveloped societies are snares commonly and successfully used. The key to successful snaring is being a patient, observant and slightly hungry human operator.

There are several models of the simple hand snare, known all over the world. Hand snares are best used when you are after small, sluggish fish in shallow water. A fish is sluggish on very hot or very cold days, directly after eating, during or after mating or spawning, when subjected to abnormal extremes in water chemistry or physical properties (unseasonal weather, industrial effluents, etc.) or when feeling generally out of spirits. In other words, a fish is sluggish for the same reasons that a human is sluggish!

Approach shallow areas in a quiet boat such as a canoe, kayak, dory, or other small rowing craft. One person paddles and navigates while the other is perched at the bow, snare in hand. Approach the fish quietly, surround the fish with the opened snare and quickly draw the snare. The fish's own effort to escape assists the snare in performing its function. Aim for just behind the head, gill slits and pectoral fins, but in front of the belly and dorsal fins.

The simplest hand snares appear below. Try using one for pinfish, pike or anything else you think you can snare.

Hand held snares

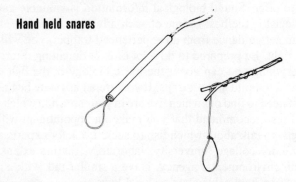

The materials include a piece of stiffened (waxed or tarred) cord or thin gauge wire and a stick or light pipe.

More complex, modern models are naturally automatic—the snarer doesn't have to wait for the fish and so is spared the daily drudgery of rigorous snare tending.

The simplest and cheapest of these complex models is pictured below.

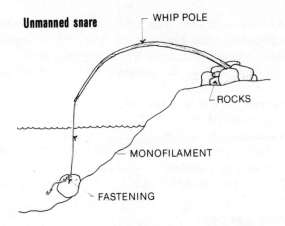

Unmanned snare

WHIP POLE

ROCKS

MONOFILAMENT

FASTENING

Fasten the line to a rock, grass or anything else secure by entangling the line or securing it with waterproof tape, another hook or a piece of very light string. The idea is to use a holding force that is slightly greater than the pressure exerted by the whip pole but less than the anticipated pulling force of the fish.

To make the snare work you'll need to experiment with the size of your hook, your bait and your location. You're likely to catch the smaller panfish using traps.

Traps and pots

Traps or pots are known from several centuries ago and the world over. The early history of this subject helps explain some facets of human development.

There are two basic kinds of traps. In one, the fish enters the trap in search of food or to hide. The internal design is such that the fish cannot easily find its way out. (The trap does not have to be as elaborate as Los Angeles to achieve this end.) The second type of trap has a springing or tripping mechanism that the fish triggers when it swims in. Few commercial fish trappers use this type, because it is too ornate and therefore expensive to maintain and prone to failure. The simple entry trap has been built in an endless variety of sizes and shapes. They can be conical, pyramidal, square, rectangular, round, heart-shaped, etc. I have seen traps 1' x 1' x 1', for tropical aquarium fish, and 6' x 6' x 4', for offshore, deep water fish. They can be

59

constructed from wood slats, wire mesh, hardware cloth, screening, pipe, plastic coated wire, bamboo, etc. They may or may not be framed. Some are weighted, some aren't. Anything goes, as long as you trap the fish. Talk to fish trappers, visit the waterfront, and experiment on your own.

Most fish traps are baited and tied to a buoy or other marker so they can be easily retrieved.

I could fill an entire book with trap designs and construction details, but instead, I'm presenting one easy-to-build, low-cost trap that is also easy to store and handle, durable, and capable of catching a wide variety of one to three pound fish. The trap plans are modified from a basic blue crab trap.

Plan for basic fish trap

The trap is 24″ square and 18″ high. A cyclindrical bait cone, 5″ in diameter and about 12″ high extends from the bottom to the *parlor.* The parlor is a layer of mesh that separates the trap into upper and lower sections.

You can build the entire box of the trap with two pieces of galvanized or plastic-coated ½″ to 2″ hardware cloth 24″ wide x 60″ long. One other piece 24″ wide x 48″ long will be enough for other details. You'll need heavy *gauge.* Gauge is a measure of the weight, size and strength of the mesh material. Hinge material, wire, nylon line and plastic rings complete your list of supplies. A ruler, wire cutters, pliers, a 2″ x 4″ piece of wood 30″ long, and a mallet, to ensure clean and even bends, are the appropriate tools.

**Plan views
of basic fish trap**

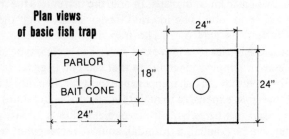

We must put some holes in the trap, to create places for the fish to enter, to remove fish, to place bait, etc. Cut two entrance funnels in the lower section on opposite sides of each other. Start one mesh up from the bottom and cut a slit about 10″ long, parallel to the bottom. Bend the slit open to 5″ wide. The entrance holes look like this:

Dimensions to trap entrance

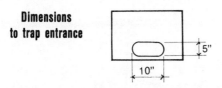

The funnels should be cut from a separate piece of mesh. Two pieces are cut, approximately 9″ wide at one end, 10″ wide at the other end and 6″ to 8″ long.

Funnel dimensions

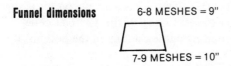

6-8 MESHES = 9″

7-9 MESHES = 10″

Crimp together two such pieces to form a funnel. The funnel is then attached inside the trap to the slit you already cut by crimping its edge to the side of the trap at the site of the split. Slant the funnel downward. Remember that you need at least two entrances on opposite sides. Four entrances—one on each side—sometimes work even better. A side view looks like this:

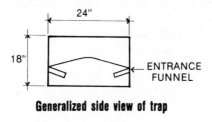

Generalized side view of trap

61

We now must cut two slits in the parlor. Most aquatic critters attempt to escape up. The theory is that when they enter the funnels, they move upward through the parlor slits and become entrapped in the upper section. The parlor slits should be about 8″ long and bent upward. You want just enough width to permit the fish to pass through. The slits are separated by four or five meshes (about 4″ to 6″).

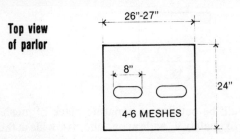

Top view of parlor

Note that the parlor dimensions on one side are 2″ to 3″ larger than the 24″ dimensions of the trap. This is because the parlor is slightly humped up in the center to rest on top of the 12″ bait cone.

The bait cone is inserted by cutting a hole in the bottom. It rests below the parlor and between the two entrance funnels. The cone dimensions are approximately 12″ high x 5″ diameter. The hole cut at the bottom will need a movable door cut from a small piece of mesh. The bait cone door is approximately 6″ square. This hinged bottom door permits you to place bait in the trap. Bait can be chicken necks, cut fish, fish heads, uncooked seafood scraps, etc. An expensive but effective bait is a can of sardines or dog food with two or three holes punched out.

The advantages to this type of bait are that the trap can be easily loaded and bait scraps, oils and others are slowly and continuously released, but it is expensive.

A cutaway side view of the completed trap looks like this:

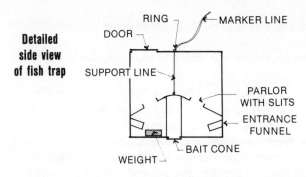

Detailed side view of fish trap

RING — MARKER LINE
DOOR
SUPPORT LINE
PARLOR WITH SLITS
ENTRANCE FUNNEL
BAIT CONE
WEIGHT

The supporting line can be light wire or nylon cord. It ties through the parlor and the top of the trap. Use a ring to connect the supporting line to the top of the trap. Then tie the marker or buoy line to this ring so the support line—rather than just the top mesh—supports the trap's own weight when you are lowering it into the water or retrieving your catch.

The top door is simply made by cutting out a square (about 8″ x 10″) and reattaching it with hinges and latches. Rubber strips cut from a tire tube, wire or ring connectors will work well. Design a door that works best for you.

You'll need a weight in a fast current or tide. It can be a rock, pieces of lead, etc., and should be secured to the trap's bottom by tying it with a piece of cord.

In summary, the trap is 24″ square and 18″ high. The parlor mesh pieces are 24″ x 26″, separate the trap into upper and lower portions and have two upward facing slits. Two entrance funnels, on opposite sides, slant downward. A cyclindrical bait cone (12″ x 5″) supports the parlor in the center of the trap. The bait cone has a small, hinged door on the bottom for baiting. The top door is hinged and serves to remove the catch.

The design presented is not absolute. You will need to make modifications to fit your local conditions and fish species. Use some common sense. Insert entrance funnels, bait cone and parlor before fastening off the top piece.

Remember, traps are illegal in some states. In other states you need a permit and must follow rigid guidelines that dictate how a trap is to be constructed and what types of fish may be caught. Check with fish authorities first.

What's most important, this trap will feed you. Good trapping!

Slat trap

The slat trap is ingenious. It was probably developed in Virginia, and works best in rivers, streams, tidal rapids, etc. It is a simple wooden rectangular box placed at an angle to the water's surface. Along the box are rows of slats that also rise off the box floor at an angle. Fish ride the rapids or tidal flow into the box and collect under a row of slats to hide, where they are trapped when the water level recedes.

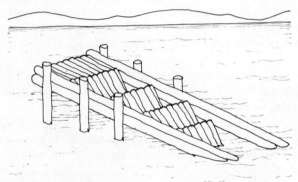

Inclined rectangular wooden box with slats makes a slat trap

Net Fishing

No discussion of survival fishing would be complete without mentioning nets. Laws governing their use and size are numerous and strict, and the subject of making and setting nets is a book in itself. Check the reference section if you are interested in reading more.

Nets vary greatly in size and intended use. Relatively small, circular bait nets and cast nets are hand held and thrown by one person. They are used in fairly shallow water off bridges, piers, and wading, usually when the fish school can be seen, and cost up to $200. At the other extreme, purse seines set from a 60′ long vessel can be obtained for the modest cost of $40,000.

Nets are always in demand, yet most commercial fishing crews don't know how to design and make them. Almost a lost art, the net makers around cannot meet the demand for nets, so if you can endure a long, hard apprenticeship, net making can be a lucrative trade.

There are, however, a few fairly simple and useful nets for functional survival fishing. Fortunately, thanks to machine sewing, you no longer need to tie a net from a spool of twine. Instead, you can purchase webbing already made so that you only need to sew the sections together to the desired shape and size.

Scooping nets

Dip nets look like the standard Atlantic Coast crab net, only bigger—usually several feet in diameter. On the West Coast they are called brail or scoopnets. Submerge the net and hold it still. When a fish swims over, quickly pull the net out of the water. The enlarged bag captures the fish as it falls to the bottom. This method requires patience and you are likely to catch only small fish that swim on the surface. Try it at night from a pier or sea wall.

Scoop or dip net

Push nets are similar to dip nets, but they have a shallow net bag with a leading (front) edge that is straight. Wading in shallow water, push the net along the water bottom. Use this net in tidal areas, marshes, creeks, small channels, etc.

A net you push

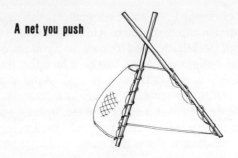

Lift nets are used everywhere in the world. On the West Coast, they are called ring nets; in Florida, they are hoop nets. They can be round, oval or rectangular, but they all have shallow net bags, are framed with wood or metal, and are supported by booms, bridles or lines.

Bait the lift net and lower it to some depth, or all the way to the bottom. It should stay in one position until you are ready to lift it rapidly, entrapping the fish that are feeding on the bait.

The lift net is best used near shore, from a wharf, pier or dock.

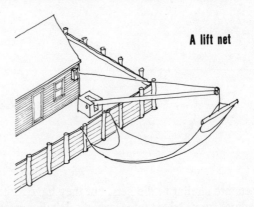

A lift net

Entrapping nets

There are many different types of nets that trap. The wade seine requires two people to wade in shallow water, each carrying an end of the net. Fish biologists often collect samples using short lengths of this net. It is most effective in shallow cuts and canals, tidal flats, etc.

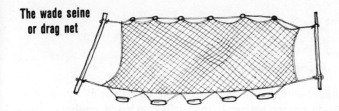

The wade seine or drag net

Hang lead weights along the bottom and if you like, floats along the top. Each person pulls by placing both hands on the poles, taking care to keep the net at the bottom.

Weirs and pounds are fixed in place with floats, poles, anchors and lines. They are large traps, constructed of netting, and they use the entire water column when the entrance is blocked off. They can hold fish alive until they are brought to market. These nets can obstruct navigation so their use is discouraged, and sometimes illegal. They are designed to guide fish voluntarily into a terminal "pocket." The following line drawing (top view) represents a net 4' to 12' high:

Pound net

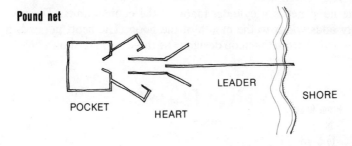

What you build is really a question of scale. Leaders up to two miles long are used by commercial crews in some areas. The basic idea is that fish swimming along shore are turned towards the pound by the leader. The heart concentrates and guides the fish. The pocket entraps them. The fish can be removed from the pocket with a dip net. The dimensions of the first pocket you attempt should not exceed 12' x 20'.

Other design patterns look like this:

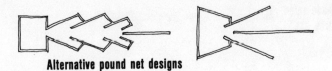

Alternative pound net designs

Experiment with design and placement, but remember that the net must extend from the bottom to the surface. Also remember to check on local laws for such nets. Since they are fixed in position, they represent a potential hazard to boats. Take care not to obstruct vessel navigation, swimming areas, etc.

The hoop, fyke and heart nets have certain advantages over the larger, more expensive weirs and pounds:

- They are made of repeatable conical net units.
- They can be small (8′ - 10′ long).
- They can be set in shallow, inshore water.
- Anchoring is easily done with crude poles or rocks.
- They are relatively inexpensive and simple.
- They catch fish.

The hoop net is a cylinder made of the conical units. The fyke simply adds wings to the mouth of the hoop. The heart net adds a leader and heart to the hoop design. The three nets are shown below:

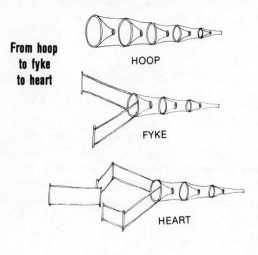

From hoop to fyke to heart

HOOP

FYKE

HEART

68

A detailed hoop net is shown below:

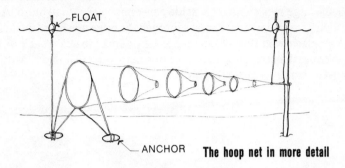

The hoop net in more detail

Entangling nets

The gill and trammel are two useful entangling nets. Both have been substantially modified over the years.

You need a boat to set a gill net, which can drift, or be anchored or stalked. The gill net has floats along the top and lead weights along the bottom. By changing the ratios of these you can float the net, sink it to the bottom, or let it rest anywhere in between. The mesh on a gill net permits the fish's head to enter, but not its middle section or belly. In its struggle to free itself, the fish entwines its gill covers in the meshes.

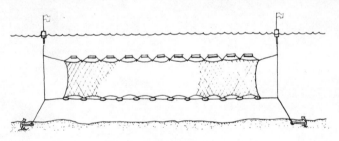

The gill net

Commercial gill nets are usually at least 1,000′ but 300′ should do for a smaller-scale effort. You can buy the net ready to fish, sew it entirely yourself, or sew factory-made webbing together. Mesh size depends on the type and size of the fish you are after.

The trammel net is a little more complicated. Three panels of webbing are suspended from the float line. The two outside panels have a large mesh while the inside panel has a very small mesh. A fish entering from either side passes through the large mesh and pushes the small mesh web through the other side. This creates a sack or bag, enclosing the struggling fish. Use this net where fish move swiftly in schools, such as at the beach.

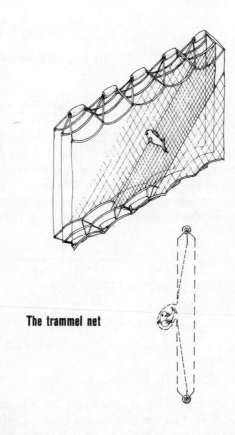

The trammel net

The cast net

The cast net is ideal in principle for survival needs. It is fairly inexpensive to buy and easy to make, can be operated by one person and produces fish for the table. The weakness of the cast net is that it can only be used in very special situations and for certain species. It is best used from a pier, bridge, wharf, or while wading in shallow flats. The history of the cast net dates back three thousand years. It originated in the southern Pacific (Malayan area) and was once used in Europe to catch birds.

There are several books which give the details of making and throwing several different designs for cast nets. A good introductory book is Ted Dahlem's, noted in the reference section.

References

"Night Stalking Flounder in the Ocean Surf." S. M. Warlen. 1975. *Marine Fisheries Review Paper 1159.*

"Commercial Flounder Gigging" (Leaflet 586). H. M. Floyd. 1966. U.S. Fish Wildlife Service.

"Fish Catching Methods of the World." A. Von Brandt. 1964. Fishing News (Books) Ltd. London, England.

"How to Make and Set Nets." J. Garner. 1962. Fishing News (Books) Ltd. London, England.

Seafood Fishing for Amateur and Professional. R. C. O'Farrell. 1971. International Marine Publishing. Camden, Maine.

Commercial Fishing Methods—An Introduction to Vessels and Gear. J. C. Sainsbury. 1971. International Marine Publishing. Camden, Maine.

Inshore Fishing. S. Judd. 1971. International Marine Publishing. Camden, Maine.

"Commercial Fishing Gear of the United States" (Circular 109). 1961. Bureau of Commercial Fisheries, Fish and Wildlife Service.

"Net Mending and Patching." P. D. Lorimer. 1976. Pacific Sea Grant Marine Advisory Program. Oregon State University Cooperative Extension Service, Corvallis, Oregon.

"How to Make and Mend Fish Nets" (Leaflet No. 125) and "Methods of Net Mending in New England" (Leaflet No. 241). National Marine Fisheries Services Department of Commerce, Washington, D.C.

Deep Sea Trawling. John Garner. Gourock Ropework Co. Ltd., Port Glasgow, Scotland.

How to Make and Mend Cast Nets. Ted Dahlem. 1968. Great Outdoors, St. Petersburg, Florida.

Net Making. Charles Holdgate. 1972. Emerson Books, Buchanan, New York.

CHAPTER THREE
In the Marketplace

Buying Fish

Ever watch people in the process of buying a used car? They kick the tires, look in the trunk, check under the hood, listen to the engine. Maybe they'll check the oil and radiator water, operate the signal lights and turn on the radio. Whether they are really capable of evaluating the car before buying it is another question. But they are following an accepted evaluation procedure, and after buying a lemon or two, they start learning what to watch out for.

The naive buyer simply doesn't know what to check or how. Car buffs and mechanics, on the other hand, aren't likely to buy a worthless car. The same principle applies to buying fish. Try learning the simple guidelines explained here and you will become a wise fish buyer.

Usually we say, "There's something fishy going on here," and we mean something seems suspiciously wrong. But if you turn up your nose at a fishy fish you'll be coming back from the market empty-handed. Fish are fishy, by their nature and definition! You must look deeper than just a fishy smell, or the lack of it, to buy a fresh fish.

A fish odor should be fresh and mild. The skin and meat color should be shiny, bright and unfaded. Flesh should be firm, never separating from the bones. Cloudy or sunken eyes may be a sign the fish has been too long out of the water.

Remember though that some fish, such as mackerels, look and smell fishy even when they are fresh. Their flesh is grey from an abundance of oils and fats. Their meat is dark and blood-filled, and their odor is naturally strong. Becoming proficient at choosing such fish takes a little practice.

Probably the most important characteristic to determine freshness in fish is the color of the gills. Gills should be a deep or bright red and free of large amounts of slime. Gills are high in blood content because that is the organ where gas is exchanged: Carbon dioxide from the fish's blood is released into the water and oxygen is taken in through the gills. Blood carries oxygen and carbon dioxide, and fades in color after the fish dies due to various chemical changes. Fresh oxygenated blood is bright red. Again, gill color varies among fish species, so you will have to learn what gill color in bluefish indicates freshness and what color indicates freshness in red snapper. But faded gill color, in general, is a sign of old fish.

The Fish Cuts

Before you can understand the secrets of making the best buy in the market you must know the various cuts in which fish are sold. The cuts will also be the basis of calculating how much fish to buy.

Some fish are available just as they come from the water. Known as *whole* or *in-the-round*, these fish have received minimum handling and are not cut.

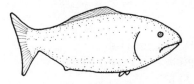

**Fish in-the-round
or just plain whole**

Drawn fish have had their entrails removed. This gutted form is probably the most common way in which fish are sold.

Drawn fish

When scales, entrails, head and fins are removed, the fish is said to be *dressed*. Removal of the tail fin is optional.

Dressed Fish

Steaks are vertical cross-sectional slices of the dressed carcass. Steaking is usually reserved for large fish.

Fish steaks

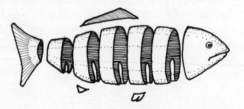

When the fleshy sides of a fish are cut away from the backbone, or rack, in one long piece of meat without bones, the result is a *fillet* (pronounced fill-ay).

Fish fillets

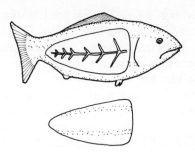

Edible Meat Yield

Take time to tackle the concept of fish yield. Everyone understands that there is waste in preparing and eating any food. By knowing how much waste to expect you can compare the various cuts to determine how much fish to buy for a specific recipe and how to make the most economical purchase.

A fish in-the-round has several sources of inedible waste. Skin, bones, head, entrails and fins are used only as food for your trees, to make soup stock, or are simply thrown away. Thus the percent edible meat yield is the lowest for whole fish, and gradually increases to the fillet cut.

Yields for the various cuts also vary with the fish species. The percent edible meat yield for flounder is much different than for salmon and both are different from the average yields the United States Department of Agriculture calculates. Don't take the USDA yields too literally: Averages are only a means of making a good general guess based on a few examples.

The USDA averages many kinds of fish species together, and offers the following yields:

Fish	Edible meat yield
Whole	45%
Drawn	48%
Dressed	67%
Steaks	84%
Fillets	100%

This explains why whole fish has the lowest per pound price and fillets the highest. When you buy a fillet the seafood marketer has borne the expense of the waste and therefore raises the price to offset the loss. This does not mean, as you shall soon see, that whole fish is necessarily the best buy.

According to this table a whole fish has about 55% waste. When you buy the drawn cut you lose almost half the weight. About two-thirds the dressed fish is edible meat; one third is waste. About 15% of the steaked fish is lost to skin and bones. And a boneless fillet is just about 100% edible.

To remind you that averages are only a guide, in-the-round Florida black mullet yields only about 30% meat. On the other hand, the Spanish mackerel yields 65% edible meat from the whole fish.

In general, a very round fish with a small, narrow head will give the best yields. A fish that bulges in the belly and has a large head and fins will give a low yield. The general guidelines here apply to all fish—freshwater, marine, large, small, flat or round.

Since yield factors are not commonly available, you may want to perform your own experiments, as seafood dealers have quietly done. The next time you buy a large number of fish or someone in your family brings back a good catch, pick five to 10 of the whole fish of one species that are about the same size. Weigh them. Now draw them and weigh again. When each fish is weighed, add up the total weight for all fish and divide this total weight by the number of fish weighed. These will give you workable averages *for that species.* Now dress the fish and weigh them. Again calculate an average by dividing total dressed weight by the total number of fish used. Finally, carefully fillet all of the fish and calculate an average fillet weight.

Assume that the average fillet weight is the average available edible meat weight for that species (100% of fillet is edible). Relate all average values obtained for the various cuts to the fillet weight to get the edible yield factors (always putting average fillet weight in the numerator):

$$\frac{\text{Average fillet weight}}{\text{Average whole weight}} \times 100 = \% \text{ edible meat yield from whole cut}$$

$$\frac{\text{Average fillet weight}}{\text{Average drawn weight}} \times 100 = \% \text{ edible meat yield from drawn cut}$$

76

Let's take an example. Assume you have 10 fish of one species. Weigh each one, add the weights and divide by 10 to determine an average whole weight. Do this for each cut, as just described. Assume you come up with the following *average* values: Whole, 10 lbs.; drawn, 9 lbs.; dressed, 6 lbs.; fillets, 2 lbs. Your calculations would then appear as the following:

$2/10$ x $100 = 20\%$ edible meat yield from *whole* fish
$2/9$ x $100 = 22\%$ edible meat yield from *drawn* fish
$2/6$ x $100 = 33\%$ edible meat yield from *dressed* fish
$2/2$ x $100 = 100\%$ edible meat yield from *fillets*

Contact the natural resources department, USDA, regional fisheries association, local fish groups, university seafood lab, local fish wholesalers or seafood retail stores for more help getting yield factor values.

Making a Good Fish Purchase

Knowing about edible meat yield is of real value when you go to the market to buy some fish. If you've got a sharp eye for weights and the loss due to bone and fins, you might be able to approximate yield factors, but until you are an accomplished fish buyer, you should calculate yields carefully.

With practice and experience, you'll be able to duel with a professional fish dealer. Of course, bear in mind the fish dealer has to make a living. Often the markup on fish is not as high as you think!

Suppose a fish market has speckled trout for sale at $.99/lb. drawn, and $1.99/lb. fillets. Which is the best buy? Lacking other yield factors for trout, you can use the USDA averages. To compare prices for the cuts of trout, calculate: *Drawn cut price divided by its yield factor equals price per pound for fillet equivalent.*

Thus $.99 ÷ .48 = $2.06/lb. for trout fillet equivalent price. Since the sale price is $1.99/lb. for fillet, the best buy is the fillets because it is lower than the fillet equivalent price calculated from the drawn price.

Suppose dressed fish were selling at $1.49/lb., and drawn fish at $.99/lb. Which is the bargain buy? Calculate: *Price of cut divided by its yield factor equals price per pound for fillet equivalent.*

Drawn: $.99 ÷ .48 = $2.06/lb. for sea trout fillet equivalent.
Dressed: $1.49 ÷ .67 = $2.22/lb. for sea trout fillet equivalent.

Note that we relate each cut to the price of fillets. In this case, the drawn cut is the most economical buy since its fillet equivalent price is less than the fillet equivalent price for the dressed cut.

How Much Fish Do I Need?

You can also use the yield factors to determine how much fish you'll need.

Suppose you have an excellent recipe for Spanish mackerel and someone in the family catches a big batch of Spanish. Do you have enough? The recipe calls for six pounds of fillets and you have 10 pounds of fish. Use the following formula: *Pounds needed for recipe divided by the yield factor of cut you possess equals pounds needed of the cut you possess.*

The meat yield for Spanish mackerel in-the-round is 65%. You need six pounds of fillets for the recipe. The mackerel is in-the-round so this is the calculation: 6 lbs. fillets ÷ .65 = 9 lbs. Since you have 10 pounds whole and need only nine pounds, you'll have more than enough to obtain six pounds of fillet for your recipe.

Suppose you have 10 pounds of drawn red snapper and want to know how many pounds of fillets to expect. Simply multiply the weight by the yield factor for the drawn cut, which is .48 according to USDA averages. 10 lbs. drawn snapper x .48 = 4.8 lbs. of edible meat. If the recipe calls for more than 4.8 pounds of fillets, there is not enough. Either cut back on the recipe, obtain more drawn fish or ask a guest not to show up.

The yield factors will also help you make other household decisions. For example by knowing your cut and weight you can decide how much fish to freeze in individual packets for future dishes.

Comparing Meat Yields

Comparing the various meat yields of fish, beef and pork is useful to determine the most economical purchases. The USDA, the state extenstion service and other sources do make studies available to the public.

If we begin with the live weight of beef, pork and fish (whole in the case of fish), we find:

- Trimmed cuts of beef are 45% of live weight.
- Trimmed cuts of pork are 55% of live weight.
- Trimmed cuts of fish are 45% of whole weight.

Herein lies a wrinkle. Trimmed cuts of beef and pork include considerable fat, gristle and bone. Trimmed cuts of fish are either steaks or fillets and are almost 100% edible. The cuts of beef or pork shrink (loss due to fat and bone) much more than fish.

If we compare yields from carcass weight of beef and pork and the analogous *dressed* weight of fish we get the following:

- Trimmed cuts of beef represent 80% of carcass weight.
- Trimmed cuts of pork represent 70% of carcass weight.
- Trimmed cuts of fish represent 67% of carcass weight.

Again a wrinkle. While it appears that beef and pork yield more, in fact they do not. The trimmed cuts are steaks, roasts, ribs, shoulders, stew meat, bacon, etc. Most of these cuts are comprised *mostly* of bone, fat, etc. The trimmed cuts of fish are entirely edible. The 23% loss in fish already accounts for loss due to bones and skin, but beef and pork cuts still possess bones and fat when you buy them. In actual edible meat, fish yield far exceeds pork and is probably superior to beef as well.

Try this experiment. Weigh your steak before cooking it and weigh it after cooking. Now remove all bone, fat and other inedible portions. Weigh the cooked meat you can eat. Do the same with a fish steak. You will note that the beef steak shrinks much more from cooking and that it has more inedible parts than fish steak. Calculate percentages and you will be quite surprised.

Consider all the steps involved as meat is processed from steer to steak. Four factors—size, shrink, service and selection—affect the price of the cuts you buy.

Size: The cost of grazing, transportation to feedlots, etc. as the steer grows.

Shrink: Dressing the live steer to carcass.

Service: Handling and transporting the meat.

Selection: Categorizing cuts and setting prices so the total sale of the steer exceeds the price paid by the retailer.

All the entrepreneurs involved every step of the way make beef a poor buy; you can thank the brokers and grocery chains for most of the problem.

If a rancher gets 50¢/lb.for steers and you pay $3.09/lb. for sirloin steak, someone in the middle is making a lot of money. Fish *never* increases six or sevenfold from producer to consumer. In 1980, fish catchers in Florida got about 25¢/lb. for their mullet, which sold in the seafood store for about 79¢/lb.—a threefold increase. Red snapper brought catchers $1.50/lb and was available to the consumer for $1.99 to $2.49/lb.—less than double from producer to consumer.

So do yourself a favor. When consumers boycotted beef and pork several years ago prices came down drastically. If you must eat beef, buy directly from a rancher, butcher it yourself and preserve it for your family by freezing, smoking, corning or brining, sausage making, salting and drying. Develop a neighborhood consumer cooperative. Buy in volume in family groups, neighborhoods, etc.

How about a nutritional comparison? While actual figures may vary between studies, laboratories, and groups doing the research, the general relationships noted below hold up. For equal portions:

	Calories	Grams of fat	Grams of protein
Steak	330	27	20
Roast pork	310	24	21
Halibut	155	7	23

The halibut, per unit serving has approximately half the calories, one-third the fat, and slightly more protein than either beef or pork.

Fish is superior to meat in many respects: It has lower producer to consumer price increases, more edible meat per pound, and it's more nutritious than either beef or pork. Only rabbit has some of the nutritional advantages of fish.

Think fish!

References

"Freezing Meat and Fish in the Home." USDA Home and Garden Bulletin No. 93. 1973

"Buying Quality Seafood." University of California Marine Advisory Publication,Marine Briefs, No. 11.

"What You Always Wanted to Know About Buying Seafood—But Were Afraid to Ask." J. C. Cato. Institute of Food and Agricultural Sciences, Food and Resource Economics, University of Florida. Gainseville, Florida.

CHAPTER FOUR
Cut It Up

Cleaning and Filleting Fish

Cleaning and cutting your fish in the desired form is a basic requirement for all fish people. When you buy beef and pork, the meat has already been cut and individually wrapped, unless you bring a whole steer home from the ranch! But after a fishing trip, or if you buy in-the-round fish, you'll have an entire fish carcass on your cutting board.

Handling Prior to Cleaning

When you buy fish in the market, it has generally been cleaned and cut for you. But if you prefer to have only your hands and utensils on the fish or if you catch your own, cleaning is up to you. Cleaning can be a big job but it is well worth it in the satisfaction it gives you, the freshness it assures you and the extra special taste.

As soon as you land a fish, take some precautions to slow the deterioration that begins the instant the fish is pulled from the water.

Deterioration through hydrolosis, oxidation and growth of bacteria accelerates with increasing temperatures. Fish high in oils and fats break down faster than others, and small fish deteriorate more rapidly than large ones. Fillets are more susceptible to bacteria than whole fish.

Don't permit your catch to flop around the boat or the beach or pier. Scars or cuts accelerate deterioration and lead to poor quality fish.

It is a good idea to bleed and gut your fish as soon as possible. Then, rinse them in lake or sea water, and if it's a long or hot day, pack them in ice. If it's a short trip, lasting only a few hours, you can get away with simply keeping the gutted fish covered, moist and protected from the sun. Do not let your gutted fish become soaked in melted ice and blood. Provide a false bottom to your ice cooler to keep your fish elevated.

Cleaning and Scaling

Rinse each fish in cold water under low pressure—hot or hard running water draws out too much of the natural juices and oils. Keep the faucet or hose running as you clean and cut so it flows continuously over your hands, knife, fish and cutting board.

Removing scales is most easily done with the dull edge of your knife, a tablespoon, or a fish scaler, but any clean metal edge serves the same purpose. Fish scalers available in most fishing supply stores for a few dollars are handy but they are not necessary. To remove scales, place the fish on its side and, holding it with one hand at the head, scrape the fish from the tail to the head, exerting slight pressure downward.

The Cutting Knife

The cutting knife, sometimes known as the fillet knife is used to cut a fish. This knife is not to be confused with the fish knife, or tackle knife, a general all-purpose fishing work knife that cuts everything from fish line to fish bait—everything *except* fish. A fillet knife cuts only fish.

The best fillet knife has a blade of at least 6″ long and at least ½″, preferably 1″, wide. Good quality steel is a must. German and Swiss knives are usually of reliably high quality, but good knives are made in the States, too.

With proper care a good knife can last a lifetime, or longer. I have a woods knife which has lasted through two lifetimes and I have every intention of passing it on to my son, in excellent condition.

But what is proper care?

Always keep your cutting knife clean, rust free, dry and stored in its own scabbard. Cutting is a continuous motion using slight pressure, and that should be all the action your knife is ever subjected to. Hacking or pounding will damage the cutting edge.

In order to cut properly, a knife must be kept sharp. If you are exerting too much effort, then it is time to sharpen your knife. Remember that the knife should do the cutting, not you. Novices simply do not sharpen their knives enough. The best way to freshen the edge, as the expression goes, is to use a stone manufactured for than purpose.

Sharpening Stones

There are natural and artificial sharpening stones. Natural stones, often called oilstones, are oil-treated during and after manufacture. Natural oilstones are very fine-grained and put a razor-like edge on a cutting tool. Natural stones come in a variety of shapes. Most have a fine and a coarse side. Pick a stone where the *coarse* side is as *fine* as you can find.

Don't let your stone get glazed. Glaze is dirt, debris, or metal particles that adheres to the stone particles. Clean your stone after each use with aqueous ammonia or an organic solvent, such as acetone, and wipe clean with a cloth. Store your stone on a flat surface away from heavy or hard objects, in as cool and clean an area as possible. Your knife will store well there too.

Mechanical and electrical sharpening stones will put an edge on your cutting knife, but they also shorten its life because they remove too much metal. And they usually leave a wire edge which is rough to the touch, rather than smooth. You will need to rework your blade on a natural, non-mechanical stone to remove this edge and put on a smooth sharp finish.

A grinding wheel is powered electrically and available wherever tools are sold. If you use a grinding wheel, it should be very fine grained, dense and have rubber, resinoid or shellac bond.

No two persons who sharpen tools agree on a single knife motion, but the following sketches depict some of the motions in use:

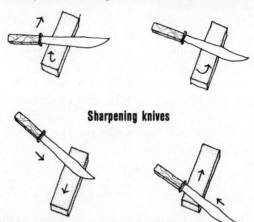

Sharpening knives

The arrows indicate simultaneous motion, not two separate motions. My choice is the motion on the top left, but use whatever works for you! Sharpen carefully and slowly.

Use similar cautions when you begin your cuts. A razor-sharp edge doesn't distinguish between fish and human flesh.

Hold the handle and place the point of the blade on a hard surface. Angle the knife about 45 degrees. The cutting and dull edges should be facing to your left and right respectively. Now exert moderate pressure on the tip. If the blade is easy to bend and bow, it is unsuitable. A fillet knife should bend only slightly.

**A test
of a fillet knife**

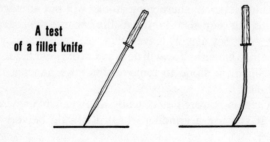

The Cuts

The fish has been chilled, scaled and washed. Your knife is razor sharp and clean. Your cutting board (commercially bought or a nice wide piece of hardwood) is wet and a steady, slow stream of cold water is rolling off the board. There is a cold beer at your side. You are now ready to perform the desired cut on your fish. Use the drawings in Chapter Three to help you visualize these cuts.

To *draw* a fish, we remove only the entrails. If you handle the knife with your right hand, then lie the fish on its side, belly facing you, with its head to your left and tail on your right. If you are left-handed, the head should point to the right. Left-handed fish cutters should reverse all subsequent instructions. All of what follows is intended for "righties."

To anchor the fish, use your left hand to exert slight pressure on its head, or hold its gills open with your fingers. Place the knife in your right hand, and insert the tip of the blade in the belly, as close to the head and gills as you can. Simultaneously, turn your wrist to face down toward the cutting board, directing the cutting edge away from you and to the right. Simply stroke the blade parallel to the cutting board, along the length of the belly toward the tail to the vent (opening on belly toward tail). Then, with your left hand, remove the entrails, using the knife to make an occasional cut to free the entrails. Wash the belly cavity with water and remove all signs of non-meat tissue (bloodlines, black tissue, pieces of organs, etc.).

Your fish is drawn. Have some beer and reach for the next fish.

There is a bit more work involved in *dressing* a fish. Start with a drawn fish. Lay the drawn fish on its back, belly pointed up. Cut vertically down from the belly directly behind the gills, as close to the head as possible, until you hit the backbone. At this point slide the fish until the head is off the board. Apply sharp pressure down with one hand, holding the belly firmly to the board with the other hand. This will crack the backbone completely. Taking your knife, complete the cut and remove the head. The head can be used in soup, chowders or to prepare stock. Or dig a hole one or two feet deep, and bury the entrails and head to make an excellent food for trees.

Now, you must remove the fins. Again, your cutting knife is the best tool. Scissors will not work because there are bones at the base of fins well within the flesh.

The large dorsal or back fin is removed by cutting into the flesh along each side of the fin. The cuts should be ½" to 1" deep and run the length of the fin. Slant the knife point inward on each cut, giving you a tapered cut that will allow you to pull the fin out with ease. The same general procedure applies to removing any other fins.

If you wish to remove the tail fin, lay the fish on its side, hold it with one hand, and simply cut the fin off. Considerable pressure is needed here to cut through the backbone and you may find it easier to use a sharp meat cleaver. You might wish to slide the fish tail off the board and use the same method to remove the tail as you used to remove the head.

Wash the fish in cold running water. Have a beer.

Steaking, which is usually reserved for large fish, requires an additional series of identical cuts on a dressed fish. Simply lay the dressed fish on its belly—or, if you prefer, on its side—and make vertical cross-section cuts at least ¾" thick. Have a beer.

Filleting fish is a high-level skill, a specialty from which some people earn their livelihood. The method described here comes straight from the docks and fish houses. It is more efficient, safer, quicker and neater than the methods recommended by the so-called experts from USDA, Sea Grant and university Food Science personnel, who have lots of book knowledge, but not much first-hand experience. Hope they will give this method a try. It takes a bit of practice to become fast and thorough.

There are some subtle differences between filleting flat and round fish. Filleting round fish is described here since that's the most common and you'll find the flat fish fillet described under *Special cuts.*

You'll be making only four cuts on each side, all in one direction, so you won't need to move the knife back and forth. Make all cuts down, or lateral, never toward your hand or body. No cuts here are blind—that is, underneath a fillet where your fingers or the blade are not visible. No other method incorporates all these features.

A few observations: The fish should be whole or drawn, but never dressed, to begin the filleting. At all times, the belly of the fish points *away* from the person doing the cutting. The first cut is always down toward the cutting board, just behind the gills, at a slight slant. The positions and cuts remain the same for left-handed people. Wrist action is as important as blade action. Finally, your cutting edge should be sharp enough to cut air into distinct, virtually visible slices!

Let's start by looking at two drawings, explained below. Each line represents a cut. It is numbered in the order you'll be cutting the fish and the direction of the cut is indicated by an arrow. Where no arrow appears, the cut is down, toward the cutting board. The dotted line is the backbone.

Summary of cuts to fillet a fish

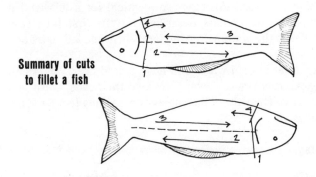

To begin the first cut, insert the tip of your blade on the other side (belly) of the backbone. The backbone hump is straight below the knife as you work a sharp edge down, see-sawing to pierce the fish. Your left hand holds the head during the first cut. But as you twist your wrist so it faces the floor and the cutting edge begins to move laterally over the backbone (second cut), you may grab the already-cut thick portion of fillet. You can now exert some upward lift to the fillet and aid the blade as it moves tailward. It is important that during the entire lateral cut of the fillet the point of the blade is reaching and touching the backbone. You'll feel it with practice.

The third cut is done using only 1″ to 2″ of the blade. No wide entrance is made into the fillet. While you are lifting the fillet upward and over, scrape the blade back across the other side of the backbone hump. If you're lucky, you will free only about 1″ of fillet on the other side. Do not try to cut more than this.

The fourth cut begins with a slanted, downward cut to meet the belly area. In one strong continuous movement twist your wrist and move the blade laterally tailward, similar to the second cut. By using the length of your blade and exerting pressure down on the bones, and with the left hand over the right raising the fillet, the cut will be complete and clean. All it takes is a little practice.

To fillet the other side, turn the fish head over tail (see the drawing), and *overlap* the right (knife) hand with the left (holding) hand. Hold the head for the first cut and as the blade moves into cut number two and frees some fillet, grab the thick free portion of the fillet and begin lifting with light pressure. All cuts are identical for a left-handed worker. Note that the process described for the first fillet (top drawing) applies to the bottom drawing for the left-handed cutter and vice versa.

Wash each fillet in cold water and have a cold beer. And don't throw the backbones (racks) away. Remove the heads, wash and freeze in quantity. Then check the chapter on cooking fish for some surprise recipes.

Special Cuts

Rib bone shave

After you've filleted a fish, there will still be from three to 12 bones in the rib cage (belly) area. Some people feel they lose too much meat by removing these few bones, but some recipes require their removal. Lay the fillet skin down, meat side up, so you can see the rib bones. Position the thick meaty edge of the fillet toward you, and the bony edge away from you. Choose a comfortable angle for the fillet. You may start at the tail (pointed end of rib bones), section A or at the wide, forward end, section B.

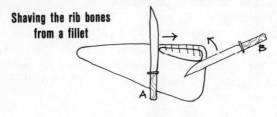

Shaving the rib bones
from a fillet

The main cutting action is to *shave* the bone section, using a slight lifting pressure. Some people simply remove this whole section with one close, angular cut. On small fish this may be preferable, if your recipe requires no bones at all.

Skinning the fillet

Lay the fillet skin side down. Proceed according to the drawing (left-handed people, angle to left and cut out to left):

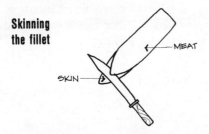

Skinning the fillet

There are two conflicting problems in removing the skin: One is the need to hold the skin securely in place (anchoring), and the other is the need to manipulate the fillet meat. Since they have only one hand available, professionals solve the problems by using a razor-sharp knife and one long continuous stroke and then not looking back to inspect the finished product.

To begin, insert a razor-sharp knife blade between the fish meat and skin at the tip of the tail, taking great care not to nick or cut the skin. Once you cut the skin you're in trouble.

Now, anchor the skin. Some people simply hold the skin and fillet together, while moving the knife. Others place an ice pick or nail in the tip of the skin, which is cumbersome and time-consuming, but useful because it frees the hand for maneuvering the fillet meat.

Once you've entered between fillet and skin, flatten the blade on the skin. Push the blade the length of the fillet, exerting a subtle, almost imperceptible, upward movement. Never remove the knife from the skin and cutting board. Occasionally you will need to wriggle the knife back and forth slightly to get it moving again.

Remember the goal is to remove the skin with only the slightest trace of meat left on it. Don't throw skins in the garbage. Like all other

89

fish parts they make excellent plant food. Some fish, such as southern dolphin (not to be confused with bottle-nosed porpoise), can be skinned by hand. Hold the fillet at its thickest corner, grab the skin and slowly pull it off with your hands. Pliers can be used to skin tougher fish.

When you've completed skinning, the occasion calls for a cold beer.

Fingers or sticks

Fingers are cut in cross-sectional strips from a shaved and skinned fillet and are usually either deep-fried or cubed for other dishes. A hefty medium-sized fish is best for this cut.

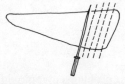

Cutting fish sticks or fingers

Cheeking or Throating

This is not a section on fish pornography. As any fish expert or restaurateur will tell you, some of the best meat comes from the head, which is normally thrown away by the uninitiated. The meat that comes from the head is called "cheeks" in the northern United States and, in the South, it is called "throats." The whole head is needed for some excellent dishes like chowders. The flavor of the fish head comes in part from the meat of the cheeks and throats.

Cheeking and throating is reserved for large fish only. When you pick up a fish head you can feel and see the areas where there is plenty of meat. Throats are cut out from inside the head. Don't be afraid to remove a few bones with the meat. There are an abundance of bones in the head and they are impossible to avoid.

Cheeks are outside the head, between the gills and the mouth. You can simply cut them out like silver dollar pieces. You may wish to skin them or simply cut out the meat leaving the flap of skin on the head. Their cooking uses are described in the chapter on preparation.

90

The Butterfly

Sometimes called the split fish, there are several methods for doing this cut, and you'll have to do some experimenting. The butterfly cut has special uses, mainly for salting or smoking any size fish or pan frying very small fish.

One method begins by removing the entrails, scales and head but not the fins. Thus you dress the fish, omitting the step where the fins are removed.

The drawing shows the next step.

Beginning the butterfly cut

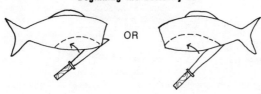

As if filleting from the belly to the back, make one long cut, staying close to one side of the backbone. Unlike filleting the cut does not go completely through. Leave a small portion of meat and skin uncut so the fish looks like this when opened:

Completing the butterfly

The dotted line is the backbone.

By removing the backbone and tail along with the dorsal fin, you'll have a double fillet, known by some as the perfect butterfly. Some punsters call it the monarch cut, taking the name from the majestic monarch butterfly. The result looks like this:

91

The perfect butterfly

Remove the backbone by making one long knife cut the length of the bones (1) and ending with a downward cut, toward the cutting board to remove the tail (2).

The finished product can almost fly

The dorsal fin can be carefully removed as described before. Be careful to leave points of attachment or you'll end up with two poorly done fillets. Have a glass of beer.

Flatfish fillet

Filleting small and medium flatfish, such as fluke, flounder, sole and petrale is slightly different from the filleting previously described for other fish. A thin-bladed fillet knife works best.

There are two distinct sides to most flatfish—a white and dark side. Oddly, the cutting technique differs for the two sides.

Holding the fish's head in your left hand, white side up and belly away, puncture the fish near its stomach but to the right of the lateral line (1). Drive the knife blade into the fish along the backbone (2) and then swing the handle down (3), using the backbone as a pivot for your knife point. Complete the cut on half of the fillet (4). Cut number (5) is down toward the cutting board. Swing the edge out toward the tail and along the remaining half of the fillet to complete the cut (6). The result is one fillet in one piece.

92

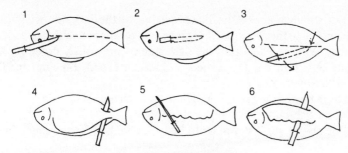

The white side flatfish fillet

A good skinning trick is to leave a piece of skin attached to the tail and flip the meat fillet over when all cuts are complete. This will serve as an anchor and works nicely on flatfish. Cut number (1) is down, through the meat to the skin. Number (2) is laterally between meat and skin. Follow the rules of skinning previously described.

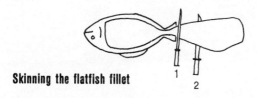

Skinning the flatfish fillet

Now turn the fish over so the dark side is up. Watch the pictures and note the direction of the cuts.

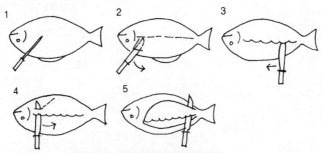

The dark side of the flatfish fillet

93

You should note that the fillet procedure on the dark side of a flatfish is identical to the first side fillet procedure for the *round* fish described earlier. You can also skin the dark side as previously noted for the white side. Leave a flap of meat and skin attached at the tail and flip the fillet over.

Don't be discouraged. You'll find that with honest practice you'll be the best fish cutter in your neighborhood.

For now, I suggest you go to bed. You've had far too much beer.

CHAPTER FIVE
Year-Round Treats

Preserving Fish

Fish is at its best when absolutely fresh. But if you are good with a fishing rod, and want to eat fish you catch through slack seasons, or a homesteader who appreciates a nutritious, hot fish stew in midwinter, learning to preserve fish is a necessity.

Preserving fish is not easy. It is the most perishable of meats and can spoil in several ways. Rancidity is the most serious. Fish meat can also turn brown, as enzymes act on certain chemicals in the flesh, and enzymes can also break down the protein in fish, releasing an odor of ammonia.

The principle preservation rule is to follow the 3 Cs: Be clean, careful and cool.

One of the basic classifications in terms of preserving and preparing is whether the fish is fatty and oily or lean. Some oily fish are herring, bluefish, salmon, mullet, sardine, tuna, whitefish, eel, mackerel, smelt and shad. Lean fish include croaker, red snapper, grouper, sea trout, bass, flounder, hake, haddock, cod, sole, turbot, small catfish, freshwater trout and freshwater pan fish.

Naturally oily foods don't dry out as easily as lean ones, so they lend themselves to broiling, baking and smoking. Simmering, boiling, poaching and frying work well on lean fish, since the cooking process adds moisture or oil to them.

Oily fish are subject to more rapid breakdown and spoilage, as explained in Chapter Four, and so should be kept in plenty of ice and stored briefly in the refrigerator or freezer. Generally, it is better to smoke fatty fish and can the lean ones.

Caution is key when you are preserving fish. The length of time you can safely keep fish varies greatly with the technique.

Dressed fish can be held for a few days in circulating refrigerated sea water, as commercial fishing vessels have done for years. Or, fish can be supercooled very rapidly, then held in a walk-in refrigerator for a long time, sometimes as long as 40 days. The key to supercooling is to freeze the cellular water in the fish flesh so the cells crystalize. The body of the fish will "give" under pressure from your finger, since it is not frozen solid, but can be kept safely in cold refrigeration.

On the other hand, there is the story of a dressed fish stored for two years in a walk-in refrigerator. Thirty minutes after his well-meaning owner fed this fish to his cat, the cat died.

So, use some common sense, and preserve away. We'll discuss refrigeration, icing, freezing, brining, smoking, salting, drying, pickling and canning.

Refrigeration

Fish will keep nicely for 48 hours in your refrigerator. Prior to storing the fish in the refrigerator, wash, clean and drain them and place in plastic bags or cover with a wrap. If you plan to keep fish longer than 48 hours, then you should freeze them.

Icing

Icing preserves fish only for a short time, unless you are using specially insulated containers, such as a fish hold on commercial vessels. Commercial fish crews and seafood handlers who know the secrets of icing can successfully keep fish on ice for as long as 10 to 14 days, but in plastic coolers or other home containers, keeping a fish more than 24 hours on ice is pushing your luck.

Begin by drawing the fish. Then put a layer of ice on the bottom of your cooler, then a layer of fish, then another layer of ice, and so on. Always begin and end with a generous layer of ice. Drainage holes at the bottom of the container should permit water to be constantly removed. Your fish should always be covered with ice but never saturated with water or slime. Insulate the containers well. Keeping fish out of direct sunlight is also important. Stuff the belly cavity of very large fish with ice.

Even though the outer layers of the fish flesh may be at or near 32°F, when fish are piled together with only a single layer of ice on top of them, the internal flesh temperature may be as high as 40°F. That is too high for safe storage and the fish may begin to spoil. The spoilage process then generates additional heat. Drawing the fish and layering the ice helps keep this problem under control.

Freezing

Prior to freezing, soak your catch in a 5% salt solution, for not longer than one to two minutes to preserve the flavor and freshness. The 5% brine is made with ⅔ cup of salt to one gallon of water. One gallon of brine will accommodate 25 pounds of cleaned fish.

You might also want to apply an antioxidant which contains the effective preservative ascorbic acid, and is available in grocery or drug stores. Follow package directions, or mix approximately four teaspoons antioxidant to one gallon of water (.5 percent) and soak the fish for one to two minutes. Be sure you are using a food grade antioxidant.

Wrap the fish in a moisture resistant covering, such as plastic bags, that will be somewhat airtight.

The USDA recommends freezing fish individually, using freezer paper and tape. Sure, that's ideal. But it's also expensive and wasteful, an unnecessary drain on the nation's resources. And some claim these recommendations stem from the USDA's conciliatory, even seductive relationship with the large corporations involved in food production, handling and processing.

Large fish should be steaked, chunked or fingered. To chunk, fillet first and then cut into desired squares. Small and medium sized fish

97

can be dressed, drawn or filleted. Never *store* fish whole since it is a waste of space and energy, and the guts are the first to rot.

Spread out your meal size packages of fish under cold temperatures at least 0°F and allow air to circulate in the freezer to freeze them as quickly as possible. Most freezers are designed to circulate the cold air. If you're freezing large quantities, it is a good idea to label the date, type of fish and fish cut with a crayon or grease pen. In addition to individually wrapped packages, fish freezes nicely in bulk quantities in water or sauces, such as tomato.

Glazing is soaking and freezing fish cuts repeatedly. Using the brine and the antioxidant solutions already noted, soak fish, and then freeze them on a tray. Don't let the fish pieces touch one another. After freezing as quickly as possible, resoak the fish briefly and place them back in the freezer. You can repeat this process several times. This forms an airtight glaze on the fish if they are kept frozen. Commercial fish dealers often glaze fish. Glazing seals the fish, locking in the natural juices and delicate flavors. Glazing prevents drying and freezer burn. Wrapping is best but optional.

There is some disagreement on how long frozen fish stays tasty. Some say most fish should be frozen a maximum of three months; others say it keeps well as long as nine months. There are no firm rules, only a few useful guidelines: Oily or fatty fish and those with grey tints to their meat color should be stored no longer than three months. The very lean, white-meated fish (red snapper, young pompano, grouper, flounder, etc.) will be good from four to six months after they're frozen. Cooked fish dishes should not be frozen longer than three months.

To thaw fish in the refrigerator, allow about eight hours per pound. Allow up to two hours to thaw at room temperature. If you thaw fish slowly, it loses liquid, so it is drier.

Cook as soon after thawing as possible. You can cook fish while it is still frozen, but I don't recommend it. If you have to, add 10 to 50 percent more time to cook it, and cook the frozen fish at a lower temperature.

Brining

Prior to smoking, salting, drying or preparing special recipes, such as fish sausages, it is wise to brine your fish. Brining draws natural water and sugars out of the meat, thus retarding bacterial spoilage. It also adds its own flavor. Brine is a solution of salt and water. A 10% brine, made with approximately one and a half cups salt in one gallon of water, works best for smoking, salting or drying. Other brine solutions are used here where appropriate.

To brine 100 pounds of fish, stir two pounds of salt into four gallons of water and soak. The brine should be saturated—that is, strong enough so that some of the salt cannot dissolve. Fresh saturated brine should float an egg on top of the solution. Always use fresh fish, and make sure it is well covered with brine.

Store the keg in a cold place with a tight lid. After about one week, remove the fish and rinse them thoroughly. Repack the fish in an empty barrel and add fresh brine—never reuse the old brine. After a few days you may repeat the process.

Rinse the fish, and then you are ready to salt, pickle, smoke or dry it.

Brining fish is never the end of the line. It must be followed by freezing, salting, smoking, canning, drying or pickling. Strengths of the brine and the length of time the fish is soaked can vary widely. A 2½% solution or a 10% solution may be appropriate, and you may brine the fish from 15 minutes to two weeks. Refrigerating the fish (40°F) is necessary if it is being soaked for a long time.

In general, the stronger the brine, the less soak time is needed. Use stronger brines for salting or drying. Use medium strengths for pickling and smoking. Use a weak brine before freezing.

Fish to be frozen needs the shortest time to brine, while if it is to be salted or dried, preliminary soaks can last up to two weeks.

There are no hard rules when it comes to brine strengths or soak times. The guidelines draw the boundaries of acceptable practice. As long as you don't step beyond those bounds, your product will be edible and, with practice, even palatable.

Some useful measures:
- One gallon of brine will soak five to 10 pounds of cleaned fish.

- Three-fourths of a cup of salt weighs approximately one-half pound.
- A salt water solution of 2½% is made by mixing one-third cup of salt to one gallon of water. For 5%, mix one and two-thirds cups salt to one gallon.
- A good general rule is two parts brine to one part fish by weight.
- A gallon of brine weighs approximately nine to 10 pounds.

Smoking

Smoked fish will last several days, or longer if wrapped in airtight material and refrigerated. Cold smoking can preserve fish for two weeks, hot smoking for up to five weeks. Of course, if you can freeze the fish after smoking it, it will keep much longer. Always refrigerate smoked fish.

Cleaning: To prepare freshly caught fish, clean the fish, then butterfly or fillet it. Some people prefer to smoke dressed fish. Don't skin it.

Brining: You must brine your fish prior to smoking it. There are three simple, but crude wet brining solutions in which you can soak the fish:

- Dissolve one and a half cups (one pound) salt in one gallon water. Soak the fish for 12 hours at 40°F.
- Dissolve four cups (three pounds) salt in one gallon water. Soak the fish for 15 minutes.
- Dissolve three cups (two pounds) salt in one gallon water. Soak one hour in refrigerator.

But I've got a secret recipe for an elaborate, absolutely delicious brine. It was invented and used for many years in the dirtiest, but tastiest smoke houses on the old Gulf of Mexico coast, and reached its peak of development on the Pensacola waterfront during the Depression and after. Thanks to Tommy Welles for sharing the brine from days of "snapper smacks and 20,000 pound trips."

From the days when fish was the basis of activity on the Gulf Coast:

Gulf Coast Smoking Brine

10 gallons fresh water
2 lbs. brown sugar
2 cups black strap molasses
4 tbls. black pepper
2 tbls. red pepper
Handful bay leaves
4 to 6 lbs. rock salt
1 can allspice (optional)

Soak 75 to 100 lbs. fish in brine for 12 to 48 hours under refrigeration. Smoke, drink, eat and make love, while you wait.

After brining, always wash fish in fresh water, rinse and let dry. Drying takes from one to four hours. You can paint on some vegetable oil at this point. A shiny, skinlike pellicle will form.

A good, functional smoker brine for about five to 15 pounds of fish and an overnight soak in the refrigerator follows:

1 gallon water
1 lb. salt
½ lb. sugar
⅓ cup lemon juice

You can also apply a "dry brine" process.

First soak 10 to 20 pounds of fish in solution of one pound salt and one gallon water for one to two hours under refrigeration. Then drain for a half hour. Mix two pounds salt with spices (bay leaf, black pepper, cloves, sage, etc.) and one-half to one pound sugar, and rub this all over the fish. Let it stand dry, overnight in the refrigerator. Finally scrub fish in water to remove the rubbing mixture and let dry for one to four hours. It is now ready for smoking. Brush on some vegetable oil.

Smoking: There are two basic smoking processes: hot smoking and cold smoking. With hot smoking the temperature rises to 200°F or more for about one hour. The hot smoke actually cooks the fish, as well as smoking it, so it will keep longer. It is usually done with larger fish and takes at least six hours. Combination barbeque and smoke cooking will achieve a similar result in one to three hours.

No direct heat reaches the fish using the cold smoke method. The temperature rarely exceeds 100° F, and requires at least six to 24 hours of smoke. For best taste results and safety, cold smoked fish should be eaten soon after completion.

Oversmoking dries fish. If you plan on smoking more than six to eight hours you should baste the fish every now and then with seasoned vegetable oil.

To really inhibit bacterial activity, using either method, the ideal is to hold the internal fish *flesh* at 180° F for 30 minutes. Hot smoking should achieve this without any problem. For cold smoking it means raising the temperature of your smoker to approximately 225° for about an hour. Saltpeter also aids in bacterial inhibition but it *has* a taste!

A smoker can be easily built and operated at home. The basic smoker requires a long, upright container with a rack or hanging device for the fish that permits smoke to travel upwards over the meat. Fish should not be touching each other. The bottom must contain either a fire or an area where the smoke can enter. Some sort of air flow control is essential. The container must hold smoke!

Small commercial smokers are now available in stores. They are functional, compact, ready to go and expensive. Many are also electric. Folks who have them say they are adequate. But to conserve energy and have some fun, build one of your own that doesn't incorporate electricity. You'll find all you need is a match to light your wood.

I have seen elaborate, homemade smokers. As long as your smoker performs its required function, there are no restrictions on size or materials. It is quite easy to construct either a hot or a cold smoker from common materials. A clean, metal barrel in good shape or an old refrigerator are excellent. A wooden barrel or box serves well, and a quick smoker can be made out of cardboard. Even outdoor fireplaces can be converted to smokers. Enclosed barbeques also work.

Whatever you use, you'll need to have an area in the side or at the bottom to permit the smoke to enter or to build your fire. Seal other holes and openings with a heat resistant, nontoxic, waterproof sealer. The hole can lead, via a conduit such as a pipe, to the fire source (a metal box, a hole, etc.). Somewhere between the fire and the container, cut out another piece that you can remove or replace in gradations. A simple slit with a removable metal plate will suffice. This enables you to adjust air flow, temperature and smoke quantities. The fire will need enough air to burn, but most of the smoke must be trapped. At the top of your container, cut out another piece so that the flow of smoke and heat will lead through the system and up.

Here are two designs for a cold smoker:

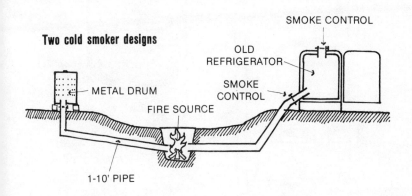

Two cold smoker designs

SMOKE CONTROL

OLD REFRIGERATOR

METAL DRUM

SMOKE CONTROL

FIRE SOURCE

1-10' PIPE

Any hardwood can be used for fuel: oak, hickory, maple, alder, pecan, apple, cherry, white birch, beech and ash are best, and fruit woods are best of all. Do not use woods containing a lot of pitch, such as pines. Sawdust and wood chips create heavy smoke.

A hot smoker is very easy to make. Here are two basic designs:

103

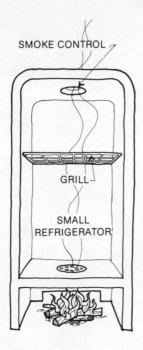

SMOKE CONTROL

GRILL

SMALL REFRIGERATOR

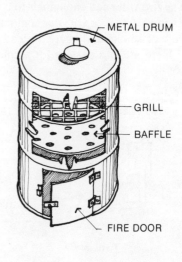

Two hot smoker designs

METAL DRUM

GRILL

BAFFLE

FIRE DOOR

The barrel can be made of wood but metal drums are much easier to find. An old refrigerator can also be used in place of a barrel.

Here is another simple cold smoker which is simply a wooden box. This general design is used to make large family smokers. In Maine, they are often the size of a shed, 4' wide by 6' long by 5' high. The one below can also be used as an excellent hot smoker by placing it on top of a metal barrel, with the fire and smoke source in the bottom of the barrel. By setting the fire source away from the smoker, approximately one to three feet, and having a pipe lead from the fire to the bottom of the barrel, you have again created a cold smoker. As you can see there are endless variations. The heat and smoke source in a shed can come from a simple metal barrel placed inside the smokehouse.

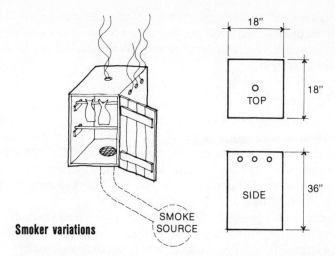

Smoker variations

Materials include plywood, scrap boards, old stove pipe and racks or dowels. Cover the stove pipe with dirt. This is a simple smoker and would serve the needs of a homestead family with no difficulty.

You can add a frill by placing the wooden box on the metal barrel. The smoke pipe should enter at the bottom of the barrel, if you use the piped-in method. This also places the wooden box at a more comfortable working height.

By doing away with pipe and offset fire you have a "hot smoker." Simply place the fire at the bottom of the barrel. A baffle (metal plate with holes in it), as shown in a previous drawing, may be necessary to deflect some of the direct heat of the fire, If you don't do this, your hot smoker is really just an outdoor broiler.

Fish can be hung in the smoker in many ways.

Hanging the fish for smoking

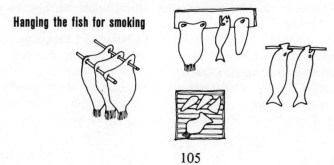

105

In smaller smokers, a last resort source of heat and smoke can be an electric hot plate with a wood chip-filled, heavy cast iron frying pan. You must watch your fuel level closely. Water-soaked hardwood chips work the best.

Salting

Salting fish is virtually a lost art in the United States, but it is still widely done in other parts of the world. In fact, cod is still salted commercially and sold throughout the world. Salted mullet and speckled sea trout still can be found along the Gulf Coast. Another impact of the revival of homesteading and survival skills may be an increase in salted fish.

Butterfly or fillet your fresh fish. Scale well, but do not skin the fish. Clean it thoroughly with vinegar and water (one teaspoon vinegar to a pan of water). Allow to dry. To salt the fish, figure approximately 35 pounds of salt for each 100 pounds of fish. Use plenty of salt—coarse or rock salt is best but any kind you can get will work, although iodized salt discolors the flesh. Pickling or canning salt works best. Use one part salt to two to three parts fish. Use more salt for oily fish or in hot weather.

Place a generous layer of salt on the bottom of a wood or a plastic container—never use a metal container. Then place an even, compact layer of fish, flesh side up, after dredging each piece in salt. Completely cover the fish layer with another layer of salt. Alternate layers of fish, then salt, until the container is almost full. Place the last layer of fish skin side up. Top off with a generous layer of salt. Place a weight over the top fish layer: A large clean flat rock or a similarly-shaped piece of wood will serve well. Cover the container tightly with a lid. Without a tight lid, moisture seeps into the salted fish. Store in a very cool place.

The curing process may take from one to four weeks, depending on temperature. The colder it is, the longer it takes to cure. To use salt fish, a good general rule is to soak overnight in clean fresh water under refrigeration. This is called freshening. Change the water frequently.

You can salt fish that is freshly cut, already smoked or even dried to preserve it longer, and add a taste popular among fish lovers. Fish that

106

is brined, then smoked and finally salted is one of my favorites. Salted fish can be broiled or baked after freshening but simmering and creaming are best.

Drying

Drying fish is widely done in tropical regions, like the Caribbean Islands. Cleanliness, along with hot and dry weather conditions, are essential.

You can dry your fish naturally, using air and salt, which is the simplest and least expensive way, but it is more prone to failure. Or you can construct your own dryer which is more complex and expensive, but guarantees you a high-quality, dried fish.

To dry naturally, begin with fresh, well-cleaned fillets or split fish. Score the meat with your knife. You may begin with fish already brined, as described earlier, or you can mix two pounds salt to five gallons water and soak 25 pounds fish for 30 minutes. Drain and air dry for 15 minutes. Use fine salt, not iodized, coarse, or sea salt, and rub well into fish meat. Now *pack,* as described in the *Salting* section, still using fine salt. Leave lean fish packed 24 hours. Leave oily fish, such as mackerel and mullet, for 48 hours.

Remove fish and scrub clean in brine soak above of two pounds salt per five gallons water. Remove all traces of dirt, salt, slime, blood, etc. Drain 15 minutes. Place fish on drying racks (wood frames with galvanized or plastic coated wire about 4' off the ground) in the shade with skin side down. The location should have excellent air drainage; downright breeziness is best! Also the humidity should be low and bugs scarce. Turn fish about four times the first day, then leave skin side down. Surround the racks with screening to keep the flies off. Bring the racks indoors to a ventilated shelter during the night. Placing fish under a press or weight at night will speed up the drying process.

During the first week of drying, spoilage can be retarded by coating the fish in salt at approximately one pound of salt for two to three pounds. of fish.

Your fish is dry when it is so hard your finger leaves no impression on its flesh after pinching or pressing the flesh. The dryer the better. If the weather is dry and warm, expect the fish to be cured in about one week, but in damp climates it will take longer.

Place dried fish in a wooden box or kep after lining it with waxed paper. Sprinkle some rock salt between layers (about 10 pounds of fish to one pound of salt). Use a good lid and store in a cool, dry place. If liquid forms, you did not dry fish well enough. If mold forms on dry fish, simply scrub it off with brine and dry it as before for another two or three days. Do the same if liquid forms.

The artificial method of drying fish replaces those airy breezes with heated air. Prepare the fish in the same way, then place it on racks enclosed in a simple box, heated from below by an electric heater or some other source. Artificial drying consumes more energy and materials than natural methods, but it works well, and also provides protection from flies and debris. Check the reference listing for more details. Food dryers are available on the retail market.

Dried fish can also be packed in moisture-proof plastic containers or bags. Store in a cold (33° to 40°F), dry place.

Pickling

Pickling, like brining, involves a solution of water and salt. But in addition, pickling also requires vinegar, spices and sugar.

It is usually a good idea to brine fresh fish before pickling. Soak fish in one-half to one cup salt dissolved in one gallon water, for about one hour. Or use one of the long-term brines recommended in *Brining* section but maintain the soak for a *maximum* of twelve hours under refrigeration.

Bring to a boil vinegar, salt, spices and sugar, then add the chunked or fingered fish and simmer for 10 to 20 minutes or until fish is easily pierced with a fork. Smelt, herring, carp, and Spanish mackerel pickle extremely well. Then pack the fish in canning containers after cooling and cover the strained boiled brine, plus fresh onion, bay leaf, etc. Pickled fish store nicely for approximately four weeks in the refrigerator (40° to 45°F).

Vinegar is the key. Use ordinary types with five to six percent acid. The final pickling solution should not be less than two and a half percent acid, or one part vinegar for one part water. Distilled white vinegar is recommended. Ordinary household white sugar is suitable.

108

Use the sugar to reduce the strength of the vinegar taste.

A good all-purpose pickle for 10 to 15 pounds of brined fish:

> 2 qts. distilled white vinegar
> 2 pints water (4 cups)
> 1 oz. each mustard seed, allspice,
>   white pepper, pickling spice
> ½ lb. onions (sliced)
> ½ oz. bay leaves
> 1 oz. hot or sweet peppers
>   (optional to taste)
> 1 clove garlic

You may then want to can the pickled fish. Techniques vary, and so do the proportions of the basic ingredients, so consult a pickling guide or cookbook for more details.

Canning

Canning fish is controversial, and there is little agreement among methods. Most publications recommend so much caution that the process becomes time-consuming, expensive and often results in poor taste and quality.

For the daring, what follows is an outline of a method suggested by the Cooperative Extension Service in Alaska. Alaskans partially rely on canned fish so they are probably the best source of information.

Cut clean, fresh, smoked, pickled or brined fish in jar-sized pieces (25 pounds of fish will fill 12 pint jars). Put one teaspoon salt in each *sterilized* jar. Fill jars to ¼" to ½" from the top with fish already cooked 10 minutes. Place jars with loose lids in a cooker with boiling weak brine for 10 minutes. Wipe the top of each jar with a clean cloth. Invert jars to permit excess liquid to drain out. Set lids in place and screw bands tightly, making certain the jars are perfectly sealed. Keep in boiling water bath for a minimum of two hours.

You can also use a pressure cooker canner, which is the safest and best home technique. Follow published canning directions. When you remove the cooker from the heat source, allow the pressure valve to return to zero by cooling down. Label and store in cool, dry place.

Trust in your own work becomes the main concern. The pressure canner is the preferred method but I do not personally recommend canning fish. If you are determined to can fish, be sure to consult some publications on canning. If you've never canned food then *don't* start on fish.

References

"Freezing Meat and Fish in the Home." USDA Home and Garden Bulletin No. 93. 1973.

"To Salt Fish." J. K. Burand. 1974. Alaska Cooperative Extension Service.

"To Can Fish." J. K. Burand. 1973. Alaska Cooperative Extension Service.

"Home Smoking and Pickling of Fish. R. L. Bradley. 1971. University of Wisconsin Sea Grant Program.

"Smoke House and the Smoke Curing of Fish." 1965. Washington State Department of Fisheries. Olympia, Washington.

"Home Canning of Fishery Products." USDA Conservation Bulletin No. 28.

'Storage of Dressed Salmon in Refrigerated Sea Water." R. J. Price. University of California Cooperative Extension Services. Marine Advisory Program. Marine Briefs.

Putting Food By. R. Herteberg, B. Vaughn and J. Greene. 1976. Stephen Greene Press, Vermont.

How to Smoke Fish. H. T. Ludgate. 1945. Netcraft Publishing. Toledo, Ohio.

"Farm and Home Drying of Fruits and Vegetables." USDA Farmer's Bulletin No. 984.

Village Technical Handbook. Volunteers in Technical Assistance, Inc. 1977. Mt. Rainer, Maryland.

CHAPTER SIX
Eat Hearty

Cooking Fish

Now, I'd like to introduce you to some new ideas and methods in fish preparation, give you some tips on some very old methods, and share with you some of my favorite recipes. My purpose here is only to tantalize you with the possibilities so you'll get yourself a good cookbook and cook away.

The secret to outstandingly tasty seafood is either very careful preservation or absolute freshness. Recipes merely adorn the most fundamental ingredient: good quality fish.

First, a note on nutrition. Fish is a very healthy food. It's high in protein and very low in fat—a combined quality that is absent in most meats.

My own diet consists of fish, fruits, nuts, vegetables, eggs and cheese—no beef or pork. But I'm not a crusader; eat what you like. The lower demand for fish keeps the price down for us fish lovers anyway.

Prior to preparing any fish dish, rinse the fish with cold water under low pressure. Steaks, fillets or dressed fish are real tasty broiled. The best baked fish are drawn or dressed. Drawn, dressed or filleted fish fry well. Use drawn or dressed fish when you want boiled fish. Any recipe that calls for cubes or pieces can be made with any of the cuts, although steaks are seldom used. Special cuts are best in special recipes. For example, the butterfly cut is good for smoking fish; fingers are good for deep frying.

Cooking Methods

Do not overcook fish. Temperature should generally not be too high, and the fish should not be cooked too long. Fish is done when it flakes easily with a fork.

Don't be afraid to experiment on your own, since a lot of cooking is a matter of personal taste! You or your loved ones may relish a dish that most people would run from.

Broiling

Place fish about 2″ below a broiling heat of at least 550°F, and baste often. Swordfish, salmon and halibut steaks, sole, bluefish fillets, herring, mackerel, trout and red snapper all broil well.

Since broiling is intense, it dries fresh fish quickly. Be sure to baste lean fish and the larger, thicker cuts often. Because fish cooks quickly, it is ideal for outdoor charcoal broiling. Broiling for 10 to 20 minutes should do the trick for most cuts of fish.

For an oily fish use a tangy sauce, such as a fruit sauce. Melted butter and lemon juice go well with most broiled fish.

Baking

Bake fish in a covered dish or wrapped in foil at about 350°F for a fairly short period. Herring, snapper, pompano, flounder, whitefish, carp, haddock and most other lean white meat fishes bake nicely. Baste once or twice, during the process.

Frying

Frying can be done in a deep fryer, or a skillet with only a little grease or in the oven ("oven-fried"). Use vegetable oils, which smoke less and impart no unpleasant flavor. When the oil temperature is about 350°, fry the fish until it is brown and flaky. Drain fish on absorbent paper. In a deep fryer, most fish will float when done.

Most freshwater fishes fry well: Fried trout and catfish are among the finest eating pleasures. Black mullet is unquestionably my favorite. Cod, grouper, dolphin and shark fry nicely.

Poaching

Poaching is an offshoot of steaming. To poach the fish, simply place it in hot liquid—salted water, wine, milk, or any appropriate combination of these—in a steamer. Cover it, and let poach for ten minutes. The liquid can later be used for sauce. (In steaming, the meat is held above the liquid, but steaming is not recommended for fish, because it reduces the fish weight drastically and leaches out tasty juices.) Check a cookbook for details on poaching. Turbot are excellent when poached.

Smoking

Smoking is not only a method of curing, but it's one of the best cooking methods around as well. The taste of smoked fish is unsurpassed. Oily and fatty fish are generally the best to use. Of the freshwater fish, carp, suckers, buffalo, catfish, chubs, trout and salmon are recommended for smoking. Many saltwater fish smoke well. I recommend king mackerel, mullet, sailfish, cobia, amberjack and eel. To my taste, mullet and amberjack are superior to all others. Experiment and you will be justly rewarded. Check the chapter on preserving fish for details on smoking.

Boiling

You'll have to talk to someone from the Great Lakes area, where boiled fish is a specialty, to learn this one. When done properly with the correct fish, it is delicious. Salt fish and lake whitefish lend themselves to boiling.

In researching this book, I went to Wisconsin to learn the best techniques for boiling fish. I found what I wanted, but unfortunately I got so drunk that when I woke up in Michigan, I found out I had lost the formula, as well as my pride. So you're on your own.

If you want to try it, bring salted water (½ cup to one gallon water) to a boil. Boil potatoes 30 minutes, onions 20 minutes, and fish 15 minutes!

Freshening Fish

To cook salt fish you first desalt it. This is called "freshening" the fish. Soak it in fresh water under refrigeration, for 24 to 48 hours,

113

changing the water frequently. Freshened fish can be fried, broiled or baked or used in soups, chowders, stews and casseroles.

Most recipes call for flaking desalted fish. To flake desalted fish, use a hot marinade: Bring 2 quarts of water to a boil, then add a bay leaf, ¼ cup chopped carrots, ½ cup chopped celery, 1 onion, 1 or 2 cloves and ½ cup vinegar or cheap white wine. Rub several pounds of fish with lemon or lime juice, then add it to the marinade and lower the heat. Simmer for a half hour. Skin, bone and flake the fish.

You can save the marinade for flaking more fish or for a poaching liquid. Don't use the mixture for another dish, such as soup. It will curl your teeth!

Recipes

Here are just a few of my favorite recipes.

Let's start with the sauces. Tartar sauce is well known, but others such as Bearnaise and Hollandaise, are excellent too. Remoulade and meuniere sauces go well with baked and broiled fish. Amandine sauce with trout is, of course, a classic. Experiment with a good fruit sauce—try it on oily "fishy" fish with a strong taste. You'll be pleased.

Pickled Mackerel

4 fillets Spanish mackerel
3 cups white vinegar
2 cups cold water
1½ cups sugar
4 tbls. crushed allspice
2 whole allspice (optional)
2 whole peppercorns
6 bay leaves
2 sliced Bermuda onions

Soak fish fillets in salt brine after removing all blood lines and fine bones. Remove from brine and cut in squares. Mix ingredients and place in jar with fish squares. No cooking. Allow to cure in refrigerator about 2 to 3 days.

Thanks to R. J. of Marathon, Florida for introducing me to this dish. Outstanding with cheese, crackers and wine.

Fried Mullet

As many fish as you can eat (Dressed, fillet, or
    butterfly)
Cornmeal
Salt, pepper, paprika

Cover fish in corn meal. Fry in hot grease. Season to taste. Lemon
juice is optional.

This dish is excellent with homemade cole slaw. The best fried
mullet and cole slaw in the world was available at Rusty's on Gulf
Beach Highway in Pensacola, Florida. Mrs. Roszak says the trick is
not to eat the slaw for 24 hours. Her simple, but excellent recipe: Mix
cabbage, onion, heavy mayonnaise, salt and pepper to taste and let it
stand one day under refrigeration. Serve with hush puppies.

Smoked Fish Dip

½ - ¾ lbs. smoked fish
1 cup sour cream or yogurt
2 tbls. lemon juice
2 tsps. chopped chives
1 tsp. onion
¼ tsp. rosemary
4 to 8 crushed peppercorns
Parsley (garnish)

Remove skin and bones from fish. Flake it. Combine all ingredients
except parsley. Chill 1 hour or more. Best fish dip I ever tasted. Serve
with crackers.

Broiled Bluefish or Red Snapper

Fish fillets
Parsley, paprika, lemon juice
Salt, pepper
Butter

Broil. (They all don't have to be elaborate!)

Trader Jon's Snapper Kabobs

Red snapper cubed
Bacon strips
Mushrooms
Lemons
Butter

According to the Trader himself, the key is to make a lemon butter with fresh lemons only. Skewer snapper cubes, bacon and mushrooms. Grill outdoors on charcoal. Baste and serve with hot lemon butter. Try your own favorite broiling fish here.

This fishmaster cook can be found any night at Trader Jon's Bar in Pensacola, Florida.

Bouillabaisse

There are many excellent recipes for this classic dish. In my view one of the very best comes from *Joy of Cooking,* by Rombauer and Becker. Many different kinds of fish can be used but I like fresh halibut, croaker or grouper best. The fish for which the dish was invented, Mediterranean rock fish, is not available in North America.

One of the really attractive aspects of this dish is that you can use the entire fish, except the entrails. The head, skin and bones all add flavor to the fish stock.

Fish and Potatoes

8 medium potatoes
2 lbs. fish fillets (Hake or cod are best)
½ lb. salt pork or bacon
4 to 5 medium onions
Vinegar
Pepper and paprika (optional)

Pack boneless fillets in heavy salt four to six hours before preparation begins.

Place potatoes in boiling water and cover until half done. Add salted fish fillets and continue boiling until potatoes are soft and fish is flaky.

116

In the meantime, dice salt pork into very small cubes. Fry slowly to render fat until brown.

Dice onions and place in covered dish with vinegar. Mash and mix fish and potatoes together. Pour some pork fat over them, then sprinkle the fried pork morsels on top. Lay onions over top. Fresh cucumbers mixed in with the onions are tasty too. Spoon on some vinegar, and some freshly ground pepper. Serves four.

To New Englanders this is a well known dish from the coast of Maine. It is also known as "Orr's Island Turkey" along that same coast.

To Mo Alexander, a lad bred on Orr's Island and an accomplished fisherman, I owe thanks for this fine dish.

Fried Fish Backs

In explaining how to fillet fish, remember that I suggested you save the remaining backbones. Remove the head and tail and then freeze a large number of these backbones. The fish backbones, with the meat you couldn't get cut off when you were filleting, are called racks; restaurateurs call them "backs."

Once you have a stockpile of these racks, dip them in your favorite batter and deep fry them. Salt and pepper to taste. Serve at least six to eight racks per person.

Fried Freshwater Fish with Hushpuppies

Freshwater panfish (Bluegills, small bass, brim,
    perch, trout, pickerel, catfish, etc.)
Vegetable oil
Salt, pepper
Flour
Cornmeal

Lightly salt dressed panfish. Place fish in paper sack with one part flour to two to three parts cornmeal and shake. Knock off excess flour and meal and place in very hot grease in deep fryer. Fish will brown all over. Keep rolling them. They will float when done. Lay on absorbent paper. Salt and pepper lightly.

To make hushpuppies, use leftover flour/meal mix from dish. Add water, milk, buttermilk, or beer. Batter should be of consistency where it sticks to a cold spoon. If you're not fully satisfied, add an egg or a little more cornmeal.

Add diced onions and lightly salt. Make golf ball sizes (or smaller) and fry in same oil as fish. Keep turning them. When done, they will float too.

Serve with baked beans, cole slaw and cheese grits. And cold beer. Thanks to Horace Carr, lifelong Agriculture Extension Agent for the advice on this southern delicacy.

Fried Catfish

Small freshwater catfish
Oil, salt, pepper, cornmeal

Catfish are good!
Tiny, little succulent fellows—
    I love 'em
Roll in meal after egg and fried hot,
Just so the fins and tails are crispy.

The meat—oh so mild and sweet!
Little lime, little salt and pepper—
    My stuff!

I learned catfish eatin' from Don Sweat, a Florida fishmaster, who can catch 'em, cook 'em and eat 'em with the best. He's not much of a poet though!

Creamed Smoked Fish

1 lb. smoked fillets
1 pint milk
2 tbls. cornstarch
Vegetables

Soak hot smoked fish in boiling water for five minutes, soak cold smoked for 10 minutes. Drain and rinse. Place in baking pan or casserole dish and cover with milk. Heat slowly. Mix cornstarch and pinch of flour in some milk or water and stir in until creamy.

Add vegetables such as potatoes, peas, carrots, string beans.

118

Leftovers are fine. Cover and bake in oven at 350°F for 20 to 30 minutes. Serve with white wine and hot French bread if you're so inclined.

From my travels along the Coast of Maine with a maniac.

Broiled Trout

Freshwater trout
Oil or margarine
Salt and pepper

Broil dressed trout. It takes about five to eight minutes on each side when placed about 3" from heat. Lemons or a tangy sauce go well with this. Brush each side with oil and salt and pepper to taste.

Common in the Northeast. Can also use small salmon or pickerel. Simple and outstanding.

Camper's Lake Fish

Any freshwater fish, especially trout
Salt, pepper
Flour
Cooking oil

Draw freshly caught lake fish (leave head on). Rinse and dust with flour. With hot skillet on campfire, using oil, margarine or bacon fat, fry fish until skin is very crisp and meat flakes.

Serve with hot biscuits and coffee. Using this simple recipe, I've had breakfast last to lunchtime.

Fish Chowder

1 lb. fish fillets
1 cup cream
1 cup milk
1 medium onion
2 to 4 carrots
½ lb. green beans
4 to 8 small potatoes
Salt, pepper
Thyme
Paprika
Margarine

Boil carrots, beans, onions, potatoes and any other vegetable you like in two cups water until tender. Fresh tomatoes or corn is nice.

Stir in milk and cream and keep simmering. Add salt, pepper, ¼ tsp. thyme, dash of paprika, sage, and basil (optional). Add up to ¼ lb. margarine. A can of cream of vegetable soup can substitute for cream. Add fish cut into pieces and cover. Simmer for about 10 minutes or until fish flakes.

While any fish can be used, the traditional "groundfishes" like cod, hake, haddock, halibut, turbot, cusk, croaker, even grey trout and whitefish are best. I learned this recipe from a Maryland seafood chef who wanted to remain anonymous, saying, "I'm not sure I should admit that chowder is that simple!"

The Simpleton's Fish Dinner for Two

2 medium size fish fillets (any kind)
Vegetables of different color (Onion, bell pepper,
    pimiento, mushroom, wax beans, scallions,
    leeks, corn, etc.)
Margarine, salt, pepper
1 cup milk

This recipe is for the bad cook who gets thrown by the delicate flavors of seafood. It also takes only 20 minutes to prepare from start to eating.

Saute vegetables in ¼ lb. margarine. All vegetables should be small sizes and just enough for two to three people. Add milk, salt, pepper, dash of white wine and your favorite other spices (don't overdo it). Cut fish in pieces and add to vegetables.

Simmer for about 10 minutes and serve over rice, noodles, pilaf, etc. Water can be substituted for milk. Serve with white wine and French bread.

The Little Known Delicacies

Sharks, skates and eels are rarely eaten in the United States, but some fine dishes can be prepared using them. Shark has been a food in Great Britain, Italy, Scandinavia and Asia for a long time and eels are

120

highly prized in Europe.

Sharks and skate have unique flavors and texture. Nutritional, like most fish, because they are high in protein and low in fat, they are a particularly economical buy because demand is low. Skate wings and steaks, and shark steaks and fillets are ready to cook when you buy them. The special problems in cleaning, skinning, treating and preserving these fish are more easily left to the professional.

And I've got a personal experience that's left me cautious: I once caught a shark, and was getting ready to bleed it. It lunged at me, and bit me solidly in the rear. The lesson will not be forgotten: Don't turn your back on a shark. Come to think of it, don't turn your front on a shark either!

Preparing Shark and Skate

Thawed, fresh-frozen shark meat must be soaked in fresh water and/or citric acid prior to cooking. Keep the water temperature at 0°F and change the water every hour, for about eight hours. Russian research indicates a 1% solution of salt or a 1½% solution of lactic 3 acid enhances the elimination of urea, which will otherwise deteriorate and give shark meat an extremely unpleasat odor and taste. For example, if the meat is left for 24 hours in lactic acid solution, the meat loses 64% of its urea. Their research also indicates that at least 12 hours of salt pickling, at 50° to 60°F, followed by 24 hours of fresh water soaking, removes most of the urea.

The "wings" of the skate are sometimes sold for meat. Many of you may have ordered scallops and been served skate by slightly unscrupulous restaurants that "cookie punch" skate wings and call them scallops. Most landlubbers can't tell the difference.

Shark and skate can be fried, baked, broiled, poached, smoked or cooked in sauce. I think smoking is best, but shark or skate go well in any recipe that calls for a sizable quantity of lean fish, and are a great substitute for meat.

Try some of these dishes and you'll be a charter fish eater.

Shark Fin Soup

1 set dried shark fins
Salt, pepper
Bay leaf
Water

The fins of all shark species work well, except nurse shark fins, which do not contain enough edible gelatin. The fins are best if taken from sharks larger than 6'. You may use the following fins: lower lobe of the tail fin; two pectoral fins (head region on the sides of the shark, behind the gill slits); and the first and second dorsal (top and back) fins. The other fins can't be cooked in this exotic delicacy.

Cook fins in a large cauldron, in hot, but not boiling water for 20 to 60 minutes, depending on their size. When white, cartilagenous platelets (tiny spots) appear at the ends the fins are cooked. Cool the fins so you can handle them, but don't let them get cold because they'll be hard to work with.

Remove the outer layer of skin under warm running water, then wash the fins in the warm water. Carefully remove the muscle and cartilagenous base.

Boil these fins gently in two parts water to one part fin for 1½ to 2½ hours. Just before cooking is complete, add salt, pepper and bay leaf to taste. The soup will have a semi-jelly consistency with many floating fibers. Serve hot and brace yourself.

Shark Steaks

Shark makes fine steaks when served with your favorite sauce. The best meat is taken from sharks less than 5' to 6' long. Some like a tangy barbecue sauce, with catsup, molasses and worcestershire sauce. A soy or tamari-based sauce is also a tasty treat.

Place your steaks in a shallow baking dish, and allow to soak in your sauce an hour or so under refrigeration.

Preheat the broiler, then place steaks on greased wire grills. Baste with the marinade sauce, and cook close to the heat for five to 12 minutes on each side, depending on thickness.

122

Skate Kabobs

I tried my first skate kabob 25 years ago at a family reunion on Long Island. And I've lived to tell the tale.

Simply chunk skate wings, and skewer them with typical kabob vegetables like onions, peppers, mushrooms, potatoes, carrots, tomatoes, etc. Use your favorite sauce or simply baste with oil, salt and pepper. Cook on barbecue grill as with any other kabob dish.

Eels

Although eels can be baked, broiled and fried, smoked eels taste best to me. Europeans and Japanese relish eels and you will too, once you try them. In a small town tavern in Wisconsin, you can order a packaged strip of smoked eel known as a "Blind Robin" along with your favorite beer. You may never return home! An epicurean zenith is a Blind Robin and a glass of mead (wine made from honey).

References

Current

"Selected Menue: Farm Raised Catfish." Catfish Farmers of America and Mississippi. U.S. Department of Agriculture and Commerce.

"Seafood Cookery Demonstration." Carolann Bowen. Florida Department of Natural Resources.

Joy of Cooking. I. S. Rombauer and M. R. Becker. 1963. Bobbs-Merrill Co. Indianapolis, Indiana.

How to Smoke Seafood. Ted Dahlem. Great Outdoors Publishing Co. St. Petersburg, Florida.

"Smoked Mullet." J. D. Lea. Sea Grant Advisory Service of Mississippi. Publication No. 970

"Don't Waste That Fish." D. R. Berg, T. M. Miller and F. B. Thomas. 1975. University of North Carolina Sea Grant publication. Chapel Hill, North Carolina

The Blue Sea Cookbook. E. Porter, ed. 1968. Hastings Publishing. New York, New York.

Fish Cookery. C. J. Davis. 1967. A. S. Barnse Publishing. Cranberry, New Jersey.

Oldies (but they could cook then, too):

Fish and Game Cook Book. H. Botsford. Cornell Maritime Press. Centreville, Maryland.

More Fish to Fry. B. Cook. William Morrow Co. New York, New York.

Delicious Seafood Recipes. L. Garrison. Crowell Co. New York, New York.

The Art of Fish Cookery. Miloradovich. Doubleday Co. New York, New York.

APPENDIX
Sources of Information

Must-See Magazines

Field and Stream
1515 Broadway
New York, NY 10036

The Fish Boat
624 Gravier Street
New Orleans, LA 70130

A national magazine covering
news and technology in fishing
industries.

Fishing Gazette
461 Eighth Avenue
New York, NY 10001

Similar to **The Fish Boat.**

Fishing News International
Heighway House
87 Blackfriars Road
London, SEI, England

Worldwide in scope.

Fishing World
51 Atlantic Avenue
Floral Park, NY 11001

Fur-Fish-Game
2878 E. Main Street
Columbus, OH 43209

Gray's Sporting Journal
1330 Beacon Street
Brookline, MA 02146

National Fisherman
Diversified Communications
21 Elm Street
Camden, ME 04843

Outdoor Life
380 Madison Avenue
New York, NY 10017

Salt Water Sportsman
10 High Street
Boston, MA 02110

Sports Afield
250 W. 55th Street
New York, NY 10019

Numerous how-to magazines such as **Mother Earth News** periodically
offer specific articles on survival fishing. Other fishing magazines concentrate
on a specific geographic region, usually a state. Ask your librarian about these.

Publishers and Government Agencies

Fish and Wildlife Service
Office of Public Affairs
Interior Building
Washington, D.C. 20240

Freshwater fishing information.

Great Outdoors Publishing
4747 28th Street North
St. Petersburg, FL 33714

Several publications on catching southern fish, especially for the beginner.

International Marine Publishing
21 Elm Street
Camden, ME 64843

Ask for their list of publications. It is a very complete offering on fish subjects.

Marine Advisory Service
Office of Sea Grant - NOAA
3300 Whitehaven Street, N.W.
Washington, D.C. 20235

Write them and ask for the address of the Marine Advisory Program in your state. Then write your state MAP for a list of their publications.

National Marine Fisheries Service
Office of Public Affairs
National Oceanic and Atmospheric Administration
Washington, D.C. 20235

Saltwater fishing information.

National Technical Information Service
5285 Port Royal Road
Springfield, VA 22161

Specialized technical information on all aspects of fishing.

Superintendent of Documents
U.S. Government Printing Office
Washington, D.C. 20402

Publications for sale on every "fish" subject.

U.S. Department of Agriculture
Office of Communication
Washington, D.C. 20250

Good information on preserving and cooking fish.

University of Rhode Island, Narragansett Campus
Marine Advisory Service
Narragansett, RI 02882

Particularly extensive collection of fishing publications.

INDEX

128